P9-APJ-687

I Don't Get It!

Helping Students Understand What They Read

Judy Tilton Brunner

ROWMAN & LITTLEFIELD EDUCATION

A division of

ROWMAN & LITTLEFIELD PUBLISHERS, INC.
Lanham • New York • Toronto • Plymouth, UK

Published by Rowman & Littlefield Education
A division of Rowman & Littlefield Publishers, Inc.
A wholly owned subsidary of The Rowman & Littlefield Publishing Group, Inc.
4501 Forbes Boulevard, Suite 200, Lanham, Maryland 20706
http://www.rowmaneducation.com

Estover Road
Plymouth PL6 7PY
United Kingdom

Copyright © 2011 by Judy Tilton Brunner

All rights reserved. No part of this book may be reproduced in any form or by any
electronic or mechanical means, including information storage and retrieval systems,
without written permission from the publisher, except by a reviewer who may quote
passages in a review.

British Library Cataloguing in Publication Information Available

Library of Congress Cataloging-in-Publication Data

Brunner, Judy Tilton, 1952–
    I don't get it! : helping students understand what they read / Judy Tilton Brunner.
        p. cm.
    Includes bibliographical references.
    ISBN 978-1-61048-002-4 (cloth : alk. paper)—ISBN 978-1-61048-003-1 (pbk.: alk.
paper)—ISBN 978-1-61048-004-8 (electronic)
    1. Reading—United States. 2. Literacy—United States. 3. Reading
comprehension—United States I. Title.
    LB1632.B74 2011
    428.4'3—dc22   2010039445

∞™ The paper used in this publication meets the minimum requirements of American
National Standard for Information Sciences—Permanence of Paper for Printed Library
Materials, ANSI/NISO Z39.48-1992.

Printed in the United States of America

Contents

Foreword

Mel Riddile

The case for improving the reading skills of each and every student has never been stronger. Whether the discussion addresses turning around our lowest performing schools, preparing all students for postsecondary education, or teaching twenty-first-century skills, strong literacy skills are absolutely essential.

Many of the nations' lowest performing schools have high percentages of under-resourced students. Many of these students do not live in language-enriched homes. These students typically enter school with a language deficit of one to two years. Without intensive reading instruction, these students never catch up. Even if schools beat the odds and successfully bring these students to grade level by the end of the third grade, these students must have direct, explicit literacy instruction each and every year or their skills will not improve. The gains made in the early grades can only be sustained through a continuous focus on literacy through high school.

In order for students to be college-, career-, and workplace-ready, they must be on-target when they arrive at high school. According to the ACT report, *The Forgotten Middle*, only 20 percent of eighth graders are actually on-target. From a school leader's perspective, when students enter the ninth grade without the requisite literacy skills, our goal for them changes from a college diploma to a high school diploma. Literacy skills will open the door of opportunity for many students.

When asked how the Microsoft University in Beijing, China, broke the stereotype of a restrictive education system to become the most productive of the three Microsoft Universities, Bill Gates responded, "You can't be creative with something that you have not mastered." Students cannot participate in honors or college-level coursework unless they have strong reading skills. Likewise, holding students who lack reading skills to high expectations, providing a rigorous curriculum, and engaging them in twenty-first-century skills is unrealistic.

I have learned through decades of experience that students cannot realize their potential without the requisite reading skills. In fact, without reading skills, there is very little that students can do in our schools.

However, there is hope. We know what reading skills to teach to secondary students. We also know how to teach students those reading skills. Most importantly, we know that teaching secondary students the right reading skills in the right way will result in dramatic improvement in student performance. When we know what skills to teach and how to teach them, there is no excuse for any school having large numbers of students who cannot read their textbooks let alone be college-ready. Our failure to treat our most critically ill education patients borders on malpractice.

Currently, only a handful of secondary schools have the capacity to implement a school wide, comprehensive literacy initiative. That means that school leaders must work to build both the capacity of individual teachers, but more importantly, they must increase the collective capacity of their entire staff to integrate literacy throughout the curriculum.

Building that capacity will require continuous, connected, and ongoing professional development supported by tools and resources. In *I Don't Get It! Helping Students Understand What They Read*, Judy Brunner provides a toolbox of proven strategies that focuses on two critical domains of researched-based literacy instruction—comprehension and vocabulary. The reality is that, without direct, explicit classroom instruction in both comprehension and vocabulary students will not progress.

When our school conducted its initial school wide diagnostic assessment, we discovered that our students' comprehension levels were higher than their vocabulary scores. That meant that our students could infer the meaning of a passage without knowing the vocabulary. We asked ourselves, what if we actually taught them the words? In addition, our analysis of our state end-of-course exams revealed that our students knew the course content but often incorrectly answered test questions because they lacked the vocabulary to comprehend the question. We came to understand that explicit vocabulary instruction was our "low-hanging fruit," and that the quickest way to improve student literacy skills in the short-run was to focus on vocabulary instruction school wide.

Our long-term strategy for raising student performance was to improve their comprehension skills. So, in addition to our school wide focus on vocabulary, we began a three-year journey to improve the collective capacity of our staff to improve reading comprehension skills.

At that time, quality instructional materials designed for adolescents were virtually non-existent. Had *I Don't Get It! Helping Students Understand What They Read* been available, we would have purchased one for every teacher and used it as a foundation for our ongoing professional development activities as well as to plan our short-, and long-term strategy to build staff capacity. This book takes away all the excuses!

Preface

MANY CLASSROOMS, ANYWHERE, USA

"Okay, kids, we're getting ready to begin a new unit of study. For our next class, you will need to read chapter 4 in your textbook. Please come to class tomorrow ready to discuss the contents."

If this classroom is like many across the United States, students will immediately begin thinking of ways to avoid the homework assignment. Some will not bother, or will only pretend to do the work. A few will read the first page, skip to the summary, and call it quits. Some may earnestly try to complete the assignment, only to be discouraged by an inability to understand the content. If the teacher is lucky, a few well-meaning students will take the book home, diligently read the material, and try their best to be prepared for the next class meeting. And in the end, only a handful of individuals will have much to offer in terms of the next day's class discussion.

Sound familiar?

Unfortunately, it probably does. Day after day, teachers make assignments, students ignore them, and both groups spend another day at school discouraged, frustrated, and bored. While principals struggle with stagnant test scores, teachers wonder how they can possibly work more diligently toward instructional outcomes.

Getting students excited about reading is possible, and it involves working smarter, not harder. Teachers need to provide direct instruction about why the material is important and must, in every way possible, prepare students to succeed. Professional development in literacy and use of the latest research and strategies helps ensure student success (Brunner, 2009).

GET EVERYONE EXCITED

Getting students excited about reading to learn really is possible. To that end, direct instruction must be provided that includes *why* the material is important and relevant, as well as how it connects to students' prior knowledge.

Care must be taken to set students up for successful interaction with the text. When knowledgeable, focused, and professional educators routinely facilitate student learning, enthusiasm will be both evident and contagious.

Whether organizing ideas, questioning authors' conclusions, making predictions, drawing inferences, or using and applying information to a variety of situations, the more students understand why they actually *need* the information, the more likely they will be to engage. All reading assignments must be relevant to the objective, and students must understand the need for—as well as their personal connection to—the content. It is the teacher's responsibility to facilitate discussion that encourages and ensures student curiosity.

EVERYONE MUST BE PARTICIPATORY

Learning to read and reading to learn cannot be accomplished at the elementary level alone. All teachers should know how to support literacy and use that knowledge to help students read, understand, and comprehend the most difficult of reading passages. It is not about *making* an assignment, it is about *facilitating* student learning through the appropriate teacher-directed vocabulary and comprehension strategies.

Acknowledgments

I am grateful to Thomas Andrews, Benjamin Campbell, Drew Langford, and Thao Anh Mai. These Parkview High School Vikings gave time and energy to help improve each reading strategy through their suggestions about technology adaptation. Facilitated by their teacher, Mrs. Nancy Wedgeworth, these student scholars provided keen insight as they considered each technique from a student's perspective.

I am also indebted to Dr. James R. Layton and Dr. Michael L. Bell. For many years these individuals served students in the College of Education at Missouri State University. Fortunately for me, I had the opportunity to learn from both of them, and their impact on me was immeasurable. Though both of their lives and careers ended far too soon, they are fondly remembered for their professionalism, integrity, expertise, perseverance, and sense of humor.

Finally, I thank my parents, Allen and Marie Tilton: In our family, higher education was not an option. It was a nonnegotiable expectation.

About This Book

Over the course of my educational career, I was fortunate to participate in a number of excellent staff development opportunities. It was evident that many subjects deserved investigation and inclusion in the vast array of topics related to continuing education. As educators at all levels recognize, knowledge of literacy strategies continues to be an area of critical need for teachers and administrators. For that reason, I decided to write this book.

As a former special education teacher and a former elementary, middle, and high school principal, one of my biggest concerns was the number of students who appeared to be disengaged from the academic environment primarily because they found reading a textbook to be overwhelming, if not impossible. I also saw many well-meaning teachers struggle with how to help those students understand, remember, and use information acquired from nonfiction expository texts. Teachers were frustrated, kids were mentally dropping out, and principals and parents were discouraged.

Whether helping a teacher during a formative evaluation, teaching university students specific methodologies, or providing on-site training for professional educators, my "audience" has always seemed to want two things:

- Strategies that are simple to implement
- Strategies that work in real classrooms with real students

With this in mind, the book is straightforward, simply written, and direct in its intention and content.

THE GOALS OF THIS BOOK

In writing this instructional resource, I hope to accomplish three things. First, the book is intended to be user-friendly. Busy professionals need to have something that can be easily referenced when they are faced with challenging and difficult dilemmas related to reading and literacy.

Second, it is important that recommended strategies not be too difficult to implement. Readers of this book will likely be from a variety of educational backgrounds; they will want techniques they can understand, and—most important—techniques they can utilize *now*. It should not be necessary for the reader to have an advanced degree in reading in order to understand and apply the contents of each section.

Third, the book should be both practical and affordable for individuals who have limited time and financial resources. Educators want strategies that are manageable in terms of time and money.

I believe this book has accomplished the aforementioned goals. The selected strategies placed within this text have been carefully considered for their ease of use, utility in terms of differentiation, and simplicity. The book can be read cover to cover, on the run, or as a resource in response to a specific need expressed by teaching staff. No matter the reason for reading the content, the book will provide practical, effective, research-based strategies to help students read, understand, and remember challenging material.

WHO THIS BOOK IS FOR

The book is for teachers and literacy coaches of all students, in all grades and all subjects. The strategies will be useful as teaching tools for a classroom with a wide range of cognitive abilities. In fact, that may be the book's greatest strength. With educator accountability at an all-time high, the use of the suggested strategies will provide a framework for meaningful instruction related to reading comprehension and vocabulary development for *all* students. The suggested strategies should produce positive results related to academic achievement and student engagement.

This book is also written for principals needing a resource for teachers struggling with how to support reading comprehension. Because reading is at the base of most academic endeavors, it is critically important that principals have sources at their disposal to help teachers differentiate and prepare for instruction in the twenty-first century. If school administrators are to be instructional leaders, they must have the tools required to accomplish the task.

This book is also for graduate and undergraduate university students pursuing teaching credentials. Regardless of the content area, the book has merit for any preservice or practicing educator who uses print as an instructional tool.

This book is also for parents. As their children's first teachers, parents want specific ways to help their children navigate the challenge of difficult textbooks. After reading this book, parents will have a number of ways to help students make the grade when it comes to reading achievement.

OVERVIEW OF THE CONTENTS

The book is divided into three sections. Section 1 includes a variety of strategies related to vocabulary. Although most reading experts agree vocabulary development is important to understanding the written word, many educators lack knowledge of specific ways that they can help students expand their personal lexicons when it comes to topics and subject areas. Teachers need to do more than merely use the glossary of a text to define a term. Teaching vocabulary is a critical component of activating a reader's background knowledge; thus, a number of vocabulary strategies are included. With few exceptions, these strategies will engage readers of all ages.

Section 2 includes a number of techniques designed to help with reading comprehension. These strategies will support students as they read fiction, nonfiction, and expository passages.

Section 3 includes information related to study skills, focusing on how students can help themselves study efficiently and effectively when a teacher is not present.

THE FORMAT

The explanation of each strategy includes discussion of the following areas:

- Why use the strategy?
- Types of texts
- Grade-level adaptability
- Levels of Bloom's Taxonomy
- Steps in the process
- Benefits
- Considerations

- Technology adaptation
- Teacher notes

Many of the strategies included in this book are applicable at most levels of Bloom's Taxonomy (Anderson & Krathwohl, 2001). However, readers should remember that the highest levels of thinking—applying, analyzing, and evaluating—occur only when the teacher consciously structures questions accordingly.

The technology adaptation for some strategies has been added for two primary reasons. First, technology is appealing to students as well as to teachers, sparking an interest when some learners might otherwise disengage. Second, the use of online resources adds a dimension to learning both vast and global. However, because many schools have limited technological assets, all strategies can be implemented without the use of an electronic resource.

MODIFICATION AND ADAPTATION

Although this book is written to provide step-by-step processes, educators must adapt and adjust the strategies as necessary. Teachers understand individual student needs and should use professional judgment in choosing methods for implementation, modifying techniques, and adapting for grade level.

It is recommended that after using a specific strategy teachers ask students for feedback related to what helped or didn't help them understand the text material. Student suggestions can be recorded in the Teacher Notes for further consideration.

WHAT THIS BOOK IS, AND WHAT IT IS NOT

This book is not the only resource educators will need as they navigate the educational challenges of the twenty-first-century classroom, but it will be an excellent beginning, middle, or final chapter in the journey.

Chapter 1

Vocabulary Strategies

There are four distinct types of vocabularies: speaking, writing, reading, and listening. The acquisition of each impacts the ability to communicate with others. While reading is the focus of this book, there is little doubt that improvement in comprehension and vocabulary development will positively affect the related vocabularies of speaking, writing, and listening.

Over the years, researchers and practitioners have learned and developed a variety of vocabulary strategies and techniques that support student literacy. Some ideas are new and some vintage—and some more practical than others. Regardless, we must recognize that some of the more traditional methods for teaching vocabulary may not work with all students. Looking up a word in a glossary, writing its definition, and using it in a sentence may not necessarily be the best choice for a lesson.

Educators must remember they are teaching students in the twenty-first century. These young people want fast-paced answers and variety of experience. Past learners may have been satisfied with a 50 mph pace, but today's students expect 0 to 100 in ten seconds or less. Though some instructional objectives do not necessarily lend themselves to instant gratification, to ignore learning styles and preferences would be less than productive—indeed, self-defeating—in today's classroom.

Each curricular area has commonly associated vocabulary words as well as other less frequently used words that are nevertheless no less important to student understanding of content. The following vocabulary strategies are well grounded in educational research and will provide variety and differentiation for students and teachers. Some of the vocabulary techniques have been modified slightly as a result of teacher input, author experience, or student suggestion.

STRATEGY: CLUSTER CONNECTION

Why Use the Cluster Connection Strategy?

The Cluster Connection strategy is designed to help students understand differences, similarities, and shades of meanings related to specific vocabulary words.

Types of Texts: Fiction, Nonfiction, Expository Text
This strategy can be easily modified for a variety of content areas.
Grade Level Adaptability: 3–8
Levels of Bloom's Taxonomy: Remember, Understand, Apply, Analyze

Steps in the Process

1. Choose vocabulary words from the text.
2. Ask students to draw a small circle including the word at the top of a sheet of paper.
3. Ask students to use a thesaurus, glossary, or dictionary to make a word web using synonyms of the vocabulary word. Students should design a cluster connection for each vocabulary word.
4. After webs are complete, ask students to pair up to share synonyms for each word. The discussion should include how synonyms may or may not slightly change intended meaning.

Benefits

• Can be done individually or with a small group
• Requires little advance preparation from the teacher
• Easily implemented by a substitute teacher
• Facilitates differentiation depending upon words provided to students
• Familiarizes students with how to use a thesaurus, dictionary, or glossary

Considerations

• This strategy may be too time-consuming to do with all vocabulary words.

Technology Adaptation

• Have students create the word webs electronically.
• Encourage the use of an electronic dictionary or thesaurus.

Teacher Notes

_____

_____

_____

_____

_____

STRATEGY: CONCEPT OF DEFINITION MAPPING

Why Use the Concept of Definition Mapping Strategy?

The primary purpose of the Concept of Definition Mapping strategy (Schwartz & Raphael, 1985) is to assist students in understanding the meaning of key vocabulary words. Through the use of a graphic organizer, this strategy will assist students with a deeper understanding of key terms.

Types of Texts: Fiction, Nonfiction, Expository Text

This strategy can be easily modified for a variety of content areas.

Grade Level Adaptability: 3–12

Levels of Bloom's Taxonomy: Remember, Understand

Steps in the Process

1. Identify key terms from the text.
2. For each word on the list, write the word on the board or have students write the word in the middle of a sheet of paper.
3. While skimming the chapter's content, students should look for the word and relevant information related to the word. Students should be encouraged to use glossaries, indexes, and the table of contents to help locate information.
4. The teacher and/or students should then create a word map of related terminology.
5. Questions to be considered while completing the map might include the following:

   What is a _____?

   What do I know about _____?

   What is an example of _____?

   How could I illustrate a _____?

   What are some synonyms for _____?

Benefits

- Encourages a deeper understanding of the term or concept
- Active involvement rather than passive memorization of key terms
- Utilizes text structure to support learning
- Can be done individually, in small groups, or as an entire class
- Applicable for a variety of subjects
- Relative ease of planning for teacher
- Prepares students for independent reading
- Easily implemented in a classroom for students with a wide range of academic ability

Considerations

- Some students may not understand some of the related words.
- Some students may need assistance in activating background knowledge related to the vocabulary word or term.

Technology Adaptation

- Students may use an electronic dictionary or thesaurus to verify the meaning of terms.
- Students may also create colorful text boxes through the use of a computer to display the Definition Map.

Teacher Notes

_____

_____

_____

_____

STRATEGY: CONTEXTUAL REDEFINITION

Why Use the Contextual Redefinition Strategy?

The purpose of the Contextual Redefinition strategy (Readance, Bean, & Baldwin, 1998) is to assist students with contextual analysis by helping them make educated guesses related to the meaning of a specific word. By using the steps in the process of this strategy, students will be better prepared to read efficiently and proficiently without teacher assistance.

Types of Texts: Fiction, Nonfiction, Expository Text
This strategy can be easily modified for a variety of content areas.
Grade Level Adaptability: Grades 3–12
Levels of Bloom's Taxonomy: Remember, Understand, Apply, Analyze

Steps in the Process

1. Select unfamiliar vocabulary words from the reading.
2. Write a sentence that includes each word. The sentence should give clues to the meaning of the vocabulary word.
3. Divide students into small groups.
4. Present individual words to groups of students. This can be done with a whiteboard or transparency, using PowerPoint, or on paper. In some cases, it may help to pronounce each word for the students.
5. Instruct students to define each word based upon background knowledge, and to be prepared to explain why the definition is correct.
6. After students have finished providing their own definitions, give each group vocabulary words in the context of how they will appear in the reading.
7. If necessary, ask students to use the sentence to modify previous definitions.
8. After modifications are made, direct students to verify definitions using the glossary or dictionary.

Benefits

- Provides a structure for teaching students how to use context clues to decode and understand challenging text
- Provides teacher flexibility and opportunity to differentiate instruction depending upon the words given to each group
- Facilitates a deeper understanding of the text
- Actively engages students in the process of deliberation
- Encourages student collaboration
- Prepares students for independent reading
- Provides a framework for a civil and respectful discussion
- Moderate advance preparation required by the teacher

Considerations

- If students are unfamiliar with many of the vocabulary words, the activity will have limited success.

Technology Adaptation

- Have small groups of students work at a computer to brainstorm ideas or consult an online dictionary.
- Through the use of a projector, display student ideas to generate whole-class discussion.

Teacher Notes

_____

_____

_____

_____

_____

STRATEGY: EXCLUSION BRAINSTORMING

Why Exclusion Brainstorming Strategy?

The purpose of the Exclusion Brainstorming strategy (Blachowicz, 1986) is to assist students as they think about words and ideas they already know related to a specific topic. It will also provide students the opportunity to explore a controversial topic while differentiating points of view and formulating opinions based upon relevant information. This strategy promotes engagement and encourages critical and complex thinking.

Types of Texts: Fiction, Nonfiction, Expository Text
This strategy can be easily modified for a variety of content areas.
Grade Level Adaptability: Grades 4–12
Levels of Bloom's Taxonomy: Remember, Understand, Apply, Analyze

Steps in the Process

1. Display the title of the reading selection for all students to see.
2. Under the title of the selection, list five words or phrases related to the topic, five words or phrases that are not related to the topic, and five ambiguous words or phrases. These words or phrases should be listed randomly.
3. Ask students to eliminate any words or phrases they believe are not related to the topic.
4. Ask students to select the words or phrases they believe are most likely to appear in the reading selection.

5. Ask students to list words they believe may be ambiguous.
6. Explain that all students should be prepared to justify their choices.
7. Assign the reading to the students and tell them that the purpose for reading will be to see whether previous selections were accurate.
8. After students have finished reading the material, facilitate a discussion of the content. Ask them to generate their own selection of related, unrelated, or ambiguous terms.

Benefits

- Easy to facilitate and implement
- Promotes student engagement
- Supports readers that may need additional teacher assistance
- Applicable for a variety of subjects
- Activates background knowledge
- Facilitates critical thinking
- Provides a specific purpose for reading the text
- Can be done individually, in small groups, or with the whole class

Considerations

- If students have little background knowledge on the topic, the discussion of terms and phrases may not be productive.
- Teacher preparation time is needed to choose appropriate words and phrases.

Technology Adaptation

- Display the chosen words or phrases with a projector.
- Ask students to e-mail choices to the teacher so that a master listing can be compiled and electronically displayed.
- Ask students to use the Internet to electronically brainstorm the terms and phrases.

Teacher Notes

_____

_____

_____

_____

_____

STRATEGY: FOCUSED CLOZE

Why Use the Focused Cloze Instructional Strategy?

The Focused Cloze Instructional strategy (Allen, 2007) was designed to introduce vocabulary words in the context of the content. It provides an opportunity for students and teacher to think out loud about the use of contextual analysis.

Types of Texts: Fiction, Nonfiction, Expository Text

This strategy can be easily modified for a variety of content areas.

Grade Level Adaptability: 1–8

Levels of Bloom's Taxonomy: Remember, Understand, Apply, Analyze

Steps in the Process

1. Select a reading passage that includes new and unfamiliar vocabulary words.
2. Leaving the beginning of the passage intact, retype the paragraphs, omitting selected words. The omissions do not need to be at any specified interval.
3. Develop a listing of possible words to fill in each blank.
4. Project the sentences on a screen for student viewing. If a projector is not available, provide each student a paper with the printed passage.
5. Explain the purpose of the activity is to help understand the importance of using context clues, sentence length, and background knowledge when reading and understanding text.
6. Working individually, in small groups, or as a whole class, ask students to predict the exact wording for each blank space, explaining why they chose a specific word by answering questions such as, "Why did you choose that particular word?" "How did you decide upon that specific word?" and "What other words did you consider?" Students should choose words from the choices provided by the teacher.

Benefits

- Can be done individually, with a small group, or with the whole class
- Requires only moderate advance preparation from the teacher
- Encourages collaboration of thought
- Helpful in a classroom with students having a wide range of academic ability
- Requires understanding and analyzing
- Teaches a skill good readers must possess
- Applicable for a variety of subjects

Considerations

• The strategy may not be productive for advanced students.

Technology Adaptation

• Divide students into groups of two to four and provide the passage electronically. Direct them to discuss the sentences and reach consensus as to what the missing word might be. Type the selected words into the electronic passage and display to the whole class.

Teacher Notes

_____

_____

_____

_____

_____

STRATEGY: FOUR SQUARE

Why Use the Four Square Strategy?

The purpose of the Four Square strategy (Lenski, Wham, Johns, & Caskey, 2007) is to help students understand and remember the definitions of new vocabulary words. This strategy will support students as they make personal connections to each new word.

Types of Texts: Fiction, Nonfiction, Expository Text

This strategy can be easily modified for a variety of content areas.

Grade Level Adaptability: 4–12

Levels of Bloom's Taxonomy: Remember, Understand, Apply, Analyze

Steps in the Process

1. Draw a square with four quadrants on a transparency or whiteboard.
2. Ask students to draw a similar square on a piece of paper.
3. In the top left quadrant, write "Vocabulary Word"; in the top right quadrant, write "Definition"; in the bottom left quadrant, write "Personal

Association"; and in the bottom right quadrant write "Opposite" or "Antonym." Direct students to do the same on paper.

4. After students have read or skimmed the reading selection, tell them to select a word from the text that they consider important for their overall understanding of the selection.
5. Have students write the vocabulary word in the upper left quadrant under "Vocabulary Word."
6. Guide students as they develop a definition for the word. Ask them to write the definition in the top right quadrant, under "Definition."
7. Ask students to consider words or phrases they associate with the vocabulary term, and instruct them to write the words or phrases in the bottom left quadrant under "Personal Association."
8. Tell students to consider words or phrases that are opposite of the vocabulary word, and write those words in the bottom right quadrant under "Opposite."
9. Provide other relevant vocabulary words or terms from the reading, and ask students to develop a Four Square for each.
10. Divide students into small groups to compare finished Four Squares.

Benefits

- Provides opportunity for individual work and small group work
- Provides a purpose for reading
- Takes little teacher preparation
- Straightforward and easy to explain and understand
- Provides a ready-made study guide
- Good activity for a substitute teacher
- Facilitates deeper understanding of the text
- Encourages collaboration
- Facilitates deeper understanding of the vocabulary word

Considerations

- This may be a difficult activity to facilitate if students have little prior knowledge of topic.

Technology Adaptation

- Use a smart board to draw the four quadrants to model the activity.
- Have students use a computer to draw a colored shapes or text boxes to use as the graphic organizer.

Teacher Notes

_____

_____

_____

_____

STRATEGY: IT'S ALL IN THE CARDS

Why Use the It's All in the Cards Strategy?

The purpose of the It's All in the Cards strategy is to help students develop the ability to learn vocabulary and associated terminology in a novel and engaging format.

Types of Texts: Fiction, Nonfiction, Expository Text

This strategy can be easily modified for a variety of content areas.

Grade Level Adaptability: Grades 5–12

Levels of Bloom's Taxonomy: Remember, Understand

Steps in the Process

1. Provide each student with 15–20 index cards.
2. Ask students to read the text and choose 10 vocabulary words (one word per card).
3. Tell them to write the word on one side of the card.
4. Split students into pairs, and ask them to trade cards.
5. Direct each student to read the respective cards and write definitions on the back of the card.
6. After definitions have been recorded, ask students to discuss the significance of each word in the context of the instructional objectives.
7. Ask each pair of students to find additional vocabulary words, and record them on new index cards.
8. Instruct each pair of students to work with another pair of students, and discuss the terms and definitions.
9. This process can be repeated until there is a group of six students.

Benefits

- Actively engages students in the discussion of vocabulary words and terms
- Provides a specific purpose for reading the text

- Applicable for a variety of subjects
- Differentiates instruction depending upon choice of words
- Provides for student choice and collaboration
- Straightforward and easy to explain
- Takes little teacher preparation
- Allows for small-group and large-group discussion
- Easy to implement
- Good activity for a substitute teacher

Considerations

- Some vocabulary words may need to be provided to students by the teacher.
- The teacher may need to monitor each group closely to ensure appropriate participation.

Technology Adaptation

None noted.

Teacher Notes

_____

_____

_____

_____

_____

STRATEGY: KNOWLEDGE RATING SCALE

Why Use the Knowledge Rating Scale Strategy?

The purpose of the Knowledge Rating Scale strategy (Blachowicz, 1986) is to provide a way to introduce unknown words to students. This strategy activates background knowledge and helps students connect new information to what they already know.

Types of Texts: Fiction, Nonfiction, Expository Text
This strategy can be easily modified for most content areas.
Grade Level Adaptability: Grades 3–12
Levels of Bloom's Taxonomy: Remember, Understand, Apply

Steps in the Process

1. Select important vocabulary words from the reading.
2. Prepare a handout for students including each vocabulary word or phrase followed by three columns labeled "Know It Well," "Have Heard or Seen It," and "No Clue."
3. Divide the class into groups of two to four students and ask them to share what they know about the topic or words.
4. Ask students to review each word or phrase and place a check mark in the appropriate column next to the word.
5. After students have completed the Knowledge Rating Scale for each word, ask them to write sentences for words listed in the "Know It Well" column.
6. Direct students to read the text. After completion of the reading, ask them to add definitions for unknown words as well as confirm or modify their previous listing.
7. If time allows, instruct students to write sentences using the remaining vocabulary words.

Benefits

- Activates background knowledge
- Applicable for a variety of subjects
- Provides teacher flexibility and the opportunity to differentiate instruction
- Provides a purpose for reading
- Connects new vocabulary to what students already know
- Good activity for a substitute teacher
- Limited teacher preparation
- Straightforward and easy to explain and understand
- Can be done individually or with small groups

Considerations

- If students lack background knowledge, it may be difficult for them to engage and participate.

Technology Adaptation

- Ask students to use an electronic table or Excel spreadsheet to make the graphic organizer.
- Have students design a PowerPoint presentation that includes vocabulary words and sentences. Encourage creativity related to sentences, color, design, and so forth.

Teacher Notes

_____

_____

_____

_____

_____

_____

STRATEGY: LIST, GROUP, LABEL

Why Use the List, Group, Label Strategy?

The purpose of the List, Group, Label strategy (Taba, 1967) is to assist students in learning new vocabulary by emphasizing word relationships. In addition to helping students understand and remember vocabulary words and phrases, it also supports the activation of background knowledge.

Types of Texts: Fiction, Nonfiction, Expository Text

This strategy can be easily modified for a variety of content areas.

Grade Level Adaptability: 4–12

Levels of Bloom's Taxonomy: Remember, Understand, Apply, Analyze, Evaluate

Steps in the Process

1. Introduce the selected topic to students.
2. Ask students to brainstorm words related to the topic.
3. Record the words in a manner that can be displayed to everyone.
4. Ask students to individually determine ways the words can be grouped together. Explain that they will be asked to share their reasons for the grouping with classmates.
5. Place students in groups of two to four, and ask them to review the words. They should reach consensus as to how best to place the words into groupings.
6. Instruct students to label each listing of words, and indicate how the words are related.
7. After categories and labels have been assigned, facilitate a class discussion of the terms and words.
8. Direct students to read the assignment.

Benefits

- Activates background knowledge prior to reading a selection
- Facilitates a deeper understanding of the vocabulary terms
- Engaging for all students in a classroom with students having a wide range of academic ability
- Provides differentiation through the choice of selected words for each group
- Allows for both small- and large-group discussion
- Encourages collaboration
- Provides opportunity for students to consider relationships between words
- Good activity for a substitute teacher
- Easy to implement
- Applicable for a variety of subjects

Considerations

- If students do not have adequate background knowledge, they may find it difficult to generate a listing of related terms or phrases.
- The teacher should be prepared to supplement the students' lists.

Technology Adaptation

- Ask each group to create a PowerPoint presentation of the word groups that will be displayed during a whole-class discussion. Use of color and electronic creativity should be encouraged.

Teacher Notes

STRATEGY: MAGNET WORDS

Why Use the Magnet Words Strategy?

The purpose of the Magnet Word strategy (Buehl, 2001) is to help students identify important vocabulary words and terms from a text. This strategy supports the understanding of key terms and the relationships that words have within a passage.

Types of Texts: Fiction, Nonfiction, Expository Text

This strategy can be easily modified for a variety of content areas.

Grade Level Adaptability: 4–9

Levels of Bloom's Taxonomy: Remember, Understand, Apply, Analyze

Steps in the Process

1. Explain to students that a magnet word represents a broad concept within the text. These words are found directly in the text in titles, subtitles, bold or italic print, and so forth.
2. Ask students to read a text for the purpose of listing key words from the reading selection.
3. After they have completed the reading, have students make a list of the Magnet Words.
4. Give students notecards, and ask them to write one Magnet Word on each card.
5. After words are written on notecards, ask students to write related words on each card. These related words can be descriptors or words that clarify the Magnet Word.
6. Divide the students into groups of two to four, and ask them to collaborate and add details or make new cards.
7. Ask students to write a paragraph using selected Magnet Words. This can be done in a small group or individually.
8. If time allows, ask students to share their writing with others.

Benefits

- Encourages a deeper understanding of the term and/or concept
- Active involvement rather than passive memorization of key terms
- Utilizes text structure to support learning
- Can be done individually, in small groups, or with the whole class
- Applicable for a variety of subjects
- Relative ease of planning for teacher
- Provides for differentiation through student choice of words
- Easily implemented in a classroom for students with a wide range of academic ability
- Provides an opportunity for students to consider relationships between words

Considerations

- Students may have difficulty recognizing Magnet Words from other vocabulary words.
- The teacher may need to be prepared to offer a listing of Magnet Words to groups that need assistance.

Technology Adaptation

- Have students use an electronic Word document rather than notecards.
- In a computer lab, display a different magnet word on each computer. Have students rotate to each computer while adding words to each list.

Teacher Notes

_____

_____

_____

_____

_____

STRATEGY: PLAY BALL!

Why Use the Play Ball Strategy?

The Play Ball strategy was designed to reinforce and review key vocabulary terms and words. It provides students a physically and mentally engaging way to learn and review vocabulary.

Types of Texts: Fiction, Nonfiction, Expository Text
This strategy can be easily modified for a variety of content areas.
Grade Level Adaptability: 4–12
Levels of Bloom's Taxonomy: Remember, Understand

Steps in the Process

1. After students have had the opportunity to learn new vocabulary words, ask them to stand in a circle.
2. Tell students they will be tossing a ball to each other. Each student will get 1 point for catching the ball and 2 points for correctly answering the question.

3. Using a soft-sided ball, gently toss the ball to a student and ask him or her to define a vocabulary term, or provide the student the definition and ask him or her to say the appropriate term.
4. Continue the game until all students have had the opportunity to participate at least once.

Benefits

- Novel activity
- Provides students the opportunity for physical activity
- Competition encouraged
- Requires little advance preparation from the teacher
- Good activity as closure or to review for a more formal assessment
- Activity can be done indoors or outdoors

Considerations

- Classroom management skills need to be evident.
- Some students will need to be taught how to politely participate in the activity.

Technology Adaptation

None noted.

Teacher Notes

_____

_____

_____

_____

_____

STRATEGY: POSSIBLE SENTENCES

Why Use the Possible Sentences Strategy?

The purpose of the Possible Sentences strategy (Moore & Moore, 1992) is to help students anticipate meaning of words before reading the selection.

Students will be asked to make predictions about the sentences they will encounter in the text. This strategy will help students verify the accuracy of their predictions while using the text to refine their predictions.

Types of Texts: Fiction, Nonfiction, Expository Text

This strategy can be easily modified for most content areas.

Grade Level Adaptability: 6–12

Levels of Bloom's Taxonomy: Remember, Understand, Apply, Analyze, Evaluate

Steps in the Process

1. List important vocabulary from the text and display them for students. If necessary, pronounce each word aloud.
2. Tell students to use at least two words from the list and make a sentence or sentences. Ask them to consider how they believe the words will be used in the text.
3. Record the sentences on the board, even if the information in the sentences is inaccurate.
4. Continue asking students to make new sentences until all words have been used or until the time is up.
5. Ask students to read the text.
6. Using the text as a reference, ask students to evaluate each previously written sentence for accuracy and make any necessary modifications.
7. After sentences have been reviewed, ask students to generate new sentences that reflect a deeper understanding of the content.

Benefits

- Activates background knowledge prior to reading selection
- Facilitates a deeper understanding of the vocabulary
- Depending on the words given to students, provides differentiation and teacher flexibility
- Provides a specific purpose for reading
- Encourages collaboration of thoughts

Considerations

- If the chosen vocabulary words are not explained adequately within the text, students may struggle completing the assignment.
- If all words selected are unfamiliar to students, they will not be able to use prior knowledge.
- Teacher preparation time is needed to choose appropriate words.

Technology Adaptation

• Use a computer lab and have each computer display selected vocabulary words or terms. Have students rotate to each computer and write possible sentences for each word or words.

Teacher Notes

_____

_____

_____

_____

_____

STRATEGY: PREDICTING WORDS

Why Use the Predicting Words Strategy?

The Predicting Words strategy (Lenski, Wham, Johns, Caskey, 2007) was designed to facilitate the use of context clues to predict text and learn new vocabulary words. It provides an opportunity for students and teacher to think out loud about the use of contextual analysis.

Types of Texts: Fiction, Nonfiction, Expository Text
This strategy can be easily modified for a variety of content areas.
Grade Level Adaptability: 1–8
Levels of Bloom's Taxonomy: Remember, Understand, Apply, Analyze

Steps in the Process

1. Select a reading passage that includes new and unfamiliar vocabulary words.
2. Retype the passage omitting the vocabulary words.
3. Project the sentences on a screen for student viewing. If a projector is not available, provide each student a paper with the printed passage.
4. Explain the purpose of the activity is to help understand the importance of using context clues, sentence length, and background knowledge when reading.
5. Working individually, in small groups, or as a whole class, ask students to predict the exact wording for each blank space, explaining why they chose a specific word by answering questions such as, "Why did you choose that particular word?" "How did you decide upon that specific word?" "What other words did you consider?"

Benefits

- Can be done individually, with a small group, or with the whole class
- Requires only moderate advance preparation from the teacher
- Encourages collaboration of thought
- Helpful in a classroom with students having a wide range of academic ability
- Requires understanding and analyzing
- Teaches a skill good readers must possess
- Applicable for a variety of subjects

Considerations

- This activity may not be productive for the more advanced students.

Technology Adaptation

- Divide students into groups of two to four and provide the passage electronically. Direct them to discuss the sentences and reach consensus as to what the missing word might be. The selected word can then be typed into the electronic passage.
- Ask students to use an online dictionary to check answers.

Teacher Notes

_____

_____

_____

_____

_____

STRATEGY: PREDICTIONS, DEFINITIONS, AND CONNECTIONS

Why Use the Predictions, Definitions, and Connections Strategy?

The purpose of the Predictions, Definitions, and Connections strategy (Lenski, Wham, Johns, & Caskey, 2007) is to help students identify unfamiliar words as well as predict the definition of the term and the connection to the text.

Types of Texts: Fiction, Nonfiction, Expository Text

This strategy can be easily modified for most content areas.

Grade Level Adaptability: 3–9
Levels of Bloom's Taxonomy: Remember, Understand, Apply, Analyze

Steps in the Process

1. Identify a key term or concept from the reading selection that may be unfamiliar to students.
2. Ask students to write the following on paper:
   - Unfamiliar Word
   - Sentence Containing Unfamiliar Word
   - Predicted Definition Based upon Sentence Context
   - Definition of Term
   - Connection to Content
   - Personal Connection
3. Ask students to fill in the sections "Unfamiliar Word," "Sentence Containing Unfamiliar Word" and "Predicted Definition Based upon Sentence Context."
4. Using a glossary or dictionary, ask students to write the definition.
5. Have students collaborate and share their ideas.
6. Ask students to work in small groups to complete the remaining parts of the form.

Benefits

- Can be used as a pre-reading or post-reading activity
- Requires active participation from the reader
- Requires only moderate advance preparation from the teacher
- Good activity for a substitute teacher
- Provides for differentiation depending upon words provided to individual students and groups of students
- Provides for thinking aloud as students discuss how answers were formulated
- Works one on one, with small groups, and with the whole class

Considerations

- This strategy may slow the reading of advanced readers.
- The activity can be time-consuming.

Technology Adaptation

- Using an online dictionary or thesaurus, have students verify definitions.

Teacher Notes

_____

_____

_____

_____

_____

STRATEGY: TEXT, ORGANIZE, ANCHOR, SAY, AND TEST (TOAST)

Why Use the TOAST Strategy?

The purpose of the TOAST strategy (Dana & Rodriguez, 1992) is to provide students an organizational system for learning new vocabulary words and terms while working at their own paces.

Types of Texts: Fiction, Nonfiction, Expository Text

This strategy can be easily modified for most content areas.

Grade Level Adaptability: 3–9

Levels of Bloom's Taxonomy: Remember, Understand

Steps in the Process

1. Choose vocabulary words and phrases.
2. Give students index cards and ask them to write the designated words on one side and the definition and a sentence with the designated term on the opposite side.
3. Have students organize index cards with words into categories.
4. Ask students to self-quiz, quiz with a partner, or repeat the words and definitions into a recording device. Emphasize to students the importance of speaking the words and definitions aloud.
5. After the session, ask students to take a preliminary test to assess how many words still need to be learned.

Benefits

- Can be used as a pre-reading or post-reading activity
- Requires active participation from the reader
- Requires only moderate advance preparation from the teacher
- Good activity for substitute teachers

- Provides for differentiation depending upon words provided to individual students and groups of students
- Works one on one and with small groups

Considerations

- Not all students learn vocabulary words at the same rate, so the teacher may need to facilitate and assist students in setting goals for learning a designated number of words each day.
- This activity may not benefit the most advanced readers.

Technology Adaptation

- Ask students to use an online dictionary for verification of definitions and possible sentences.

Teacher Notes

_____

_____

_____

_____

_____

STRATEGY: TRAVELING TO A DIFFERENT BEAT

Why Use the Traveling to a Different Beat Strategy?

The purpose of the Traveling to a Different Beat strategy is to utilize a novel way of reviewing key vocabulary words and terms. It gives students the opportunity to listen to fast-paced music while moving around the room.

Types of Texts: Fiction, Nonfiction, Expository Text

This strategy can be easily modified for a variety of content areas.

Grade Level Adaptability: 6–12

Levels of Bloom's Taxonomy: Remember, Understand

Steps in the Process

1. Provide text for students to read.
2. Tell students that the purpose for reading the selection is to locate important vocabulary words. Explain that they should be prepared to discuss the definition and significance of the words or terms with classmates.

3. After reading the selection, students should write a designated number of vocabulary words or terms with definitions from the reading.
4. Tell students that they will be moving around the room with their vocabulary cards as the music plays. This works best when the music is relatively fast-paced.
5. When the music stops, tell students to find someone standing in close proximity and explain the definition and significance of the vocabulary word.
6. When they are provided additional vocabulary words from others, tell students to add these new words to additional cards.
7. Instruct students not to speak with anyone more than once during the activity.
8. The activity should continue until all students have had the opportunity to speak with several classmates.

Benefits

- Provides a purpose for reading
- Takes little teacher preparation
- Encourages active learning
- Straightforward and easy to explain and understand
- Provides novelty for closure
- Can be done as a culminating activity for a unit or as a review for a more formal assessment
- Enjoyable for students

Considerations

- This strategy requires space for students to move throughout the classroom.
- Classroom management skills must be evident.

Technology Adaptation

- Have students recommend a musical selection. The music should be fast-paced, with appropriate lyrics.

Teacher Notes

_____

_____

_____

_____

_____

STRATEGY: VOCABULARY CHART

Why Use the Vocabulary Chart Strategy?

The Vocabulary Chart strategy was designed to encourage students to think about vocabulary words they already know and to associate the words with a specific topic.

Types of Texts: Fiction, Nonfiction, Expository Text

This strategy can be easily modified for a variety of content areas.

Grade Level Adaptability: 3–12

Levels of Bloom's Taxonomy: Remember, Understand, Apply

Steps in the Process

1. Introduce the topic of the reading passage to students.
2. Using paper, ask students to divide it vertically into two columns of equal size.
3. At the top of the column on the left, ask students to write the heading "Words I Know." At the top of the column on the right, tell them to write the heading "New Words."
4. Prior to reading the assigned text, ask students to brainstorm vocabulary words they already know related to the topic, and to record the words in the column on the left, "Words I Know."
5. After reading the passage, have students list in the "New Words" column new vocabulary words that they encountered in the reading. Direct students to pay particular attention to words in bold or italicized print, as well as to words contained in captions to a graphic and words within a title or subtitle.
6. Students should continue listing terms until they have written several new words.
7. Ask students to work individually or in small groups to define the new vocabulary words. The definition should include how and why the words are significant as related to the overall subject of the reading.

Benefits

- Can be done individually, with a small group, or with the whole class
- Requires little advance preparation from the teacher
- Provides a ready-made study guide of vocabulary words
- Sets a specific purpose for reading
- Good activity for a substitute teacher

Considerations

- If students lack initial background knowledge of the topic, additional discussion may need to occur prior to having them read the text.

Technology Adaptation

- Ask students to make a chart electronically using graphics, clip art, or symbols.

Teacher Notes

_____

_____

_____

_____

_____

STRATEGY: VOCABULARY SELF-COLLECTION

Why Use the Vocabulary Self-Collection Strategy?

The purpose of the Vocabulary Self-Collection strategy (Haggard, 1986) is to support the growth of general and specific content vocabulary related to a topic of subject by allowing students to choose important vocabulary words from the reading passage.

Types of Texts: Fiction, Nonfiction, Expository Text

This strategy can be easily modified for a variety of content areas.

Grade Level Adaptability: 4–12

Levels of Bloom's Taxonomy: Remember, Understand, Analyze, Evaluate

Steps in the Process

1. Ask students to complete a reading assignment from the text.
2. Place students into groups of two to four and have them review the reading selection for the purpose of identifying vocabulary words, terms, or concepts they believe are important to the overall understanding of the content.
3. Record words and discuss them with students.

4. Ask groups of students to share selections, and to display the word selection to the whole class.
5. Facilitate discussion related to the importance of individual words. If necessary, be prepared to add words to the students' lists.
6. As words are recorded, ask students to provide definitions.
7. Ask students to place the vocabulary words and definitions in a personal vocabulary list.

Benefits

- Novelty of choice related to vocabulary words
- Straightforward, easy to explain and understand
- Appropriate for a pre-reading or post-reading activity
- Can be used to activate background knowledge
- Provides for differentiation depending upon words selected by and provided to the students

Considerations

- Student selection may not result in words that are most important to the overall instructional objectives.
- This activity can be time-consuming and might not be productive for all students.

Technology Adaptation

- Ask students to display the collection of words with their definitions electronically.
- Ask students to e-mail word lists with definitions to others in the class. After all students have had the opportunity to review lists, ask them to compile a master list of the most relevant vocabulary words and definitions.

Teacher Notes

_____

_____

_____

_____

_____

STRATEGY: WHAT'S IN A NAME?

Why Use the What's in a Name Strategy?

The What's in a Name strategy is designed to teach students how to use a thesaurus, dictionary, and glossary as reference tools. Students need to routinely use these resources. This strategy facilitates familiarity with each.

Types of Texts: Fiction, Nonfiction, Expository Text
This strategy can be easily modified for a variety of content areas.
Grade Level Adaptability: 3–8
Levels of Bloom's Taxonomy: Remember, Understand

Steps in the Process

1. Choose vocabulary words from the text.
2. Ask students to draw a web graphic organizer.
3. Direct students to write the vocabulary words in the middle of the web with at least six to eight lines extending from the circle.
4. Ask students to use a thesaurus, glossary, or dictionary to complete the web with words closely related to the vocabulary word in the circle.
5. After webs are complete, ask students to collaborate and write sentences that explain the meaning of each vocabulary word.

Benefits

- Can be done individually or with a small group
- Requires little advance preparation from the teacher
- Easily implemented by a substitute teacher
- Facilitates differentiation depending upon words provided to individual students
- Provides an opportunity to practice an important reading skill

Considerations

- This strategy may be too time-consuming to do with all vocabulary words.
- The activity may be too laborious for advanced readers.

Technology Adaptation

- Have students create the word webs electronically.
- Encourage the use of an electronic dictionary or thesaurus.

Teacher Notes

_____

_____

_____

_____

_____

STRATEGY: WORD O

Why Use the Wordo Strategy?

The purpose of the Wordo strategy (Rasinski and Padak, 2004) is to provide a competitive and novel way of reviewing content vocabulary words.

Types of Texts: Fiction, Nonfiction, Expository Text

This strategy can be easily modified for a variety of content areas.

Grade Level Adaptability: 3–12

Levels of Bloom's Taxonomy: Remember, Understand

Steps in the Process

1. Tell students they will play a game similar to Bingo.
2. Choose 24 vocabulary words and have students write each word randomly on a Bingo-type card.
3. Select one word at a time and provide the definition, a synonym, an antonym, or other clue to the word.
4. Tell players they must figure out the word from the clue and cover the word on their scorecard.
5. Explain that the first student to cover a horizontal, vertical, or diagonal line will win the game.

Benefits

- Supports competitive spirit of students
- Novel way of reviewing key terms and concepts
- Provides teacher flexibility with vocabulary words
- Actively engages students in a game
- Student enjoyment of the activity
- Easily implemented
- Good activity for substitute teacher

Considerations

- If more than 24 terms need to be included, students will need to make several cards.

Technology Adaptation:

- Have students create cards electronically.

Teacher Notes

_____

_____

_____

_____

_____

STRATEGY: WORD PUZZLE

Why Use the Word Puzzle Strategy?

The purpose of the Word Puzzle strategy (Oczkus, 2004) is to help students analyze the meaning, draw analogies, and examine other aspects of the word such as spelling, pronunciation, and so forth.

Types of Texts: Fiction, Nonfiction, Expository Text
This strategy can be easily modified for most content areas.
Grade Level Adaptability: 3–9
Levels of Bloom's Taxonomy: Remember, Understand, Apply, Analyze

Steps in the Process

1. On a sheet of paper ask students to write the following directions:
   - Write a sentence from the text
   - List three examples of the word
   - Write the word using unusual or fancy letters
   - Make a drawing to illustrate the word
   - Write an acrostic for the word (using the letters of the word)
   - Write two important things about the word
   - Identify a key term or concept from the reading selection that may be unfamiliar to students.

2. Introduce vocabulary words and ask students to follow the directions on their paper and complete a puzzle for each word.

Benefits

- Can be used as a pre-reading or post-reading activity
- Requires active participation from the reader
- Requires only moderate advance preparation from the teacher
- Good activity for substitute teachers
- Provides for differentiation depending upon words provided to individual students and groups of students
- Provides for "thinking aloud" as students discuss how answers were formulated
- Works one on one, with small groups, and with the whole class

Considerations

- This strategy may slow the reading of advanced readers.
- The activity may be too time-consuming.

Technology Adaptation

- Using an online dictionary or thesaurus, have students verify definitions.
- Ask students to make an electronic puzzle for each word that can be displayed for the whole class.

Teacher Notes

_____

_____

_____

_____

STRATEGY: WORD QUESTIONING

Why Use the Word Questioning Strategy?

The purpose of the Word Questioning strategy (Allen, 1999) is to give students exposure to vocabulary at all levels of Bloom's Taxonomy. The questions provided to students will facilitate a deeper understanding of the vocabulary word or concept.

Types of Texts: Fiction, Nonfiction, Expository Text
This strategy can be easily modified for a variety of content areas.
Grade Level Adaptability: 3–12
Levels of Bloom's Taxonomy: Remember, Understand, Apply, Evaluate, Analyze

Steps in the Process

1. Ask students to write the following on a sheet of paper.
   * What is a sentence using the word?
   * What are the parts of the word I recognize?
   * What does the word mean?
   * What is an example for the word?
   * What is not an example for the word?
   * How does the word go with other words or concepts I know?
   * What might I be reading about when I find this word?
   * Why is this word important for me to know?
2. Provide the selected vocabulary word to the students and ask them to locate the word in the reading passage.
3. Ask students to write the sentence with the vocabulary term on the appropriate part of the paper and direct them to continue to answer the questions from the paper.

Benefits

* Takes little teacher preparation
* Straightforward and easy to explain and understand
* Requires students to think beyond the text
* Can be done individually or in small groups
* Symbols or visual images can be used to answer the questions
* Promotes a deeper understanding of the meaning of the vocabulary words

Considerations

* If students lack background knowledge, the strategy may not be effective.

Technology Adaptation

* In a computer lab, display different questions on each computer. Have students rotate through the lab answering one question on each computer. At the end of the session, place one or more students at each computer and ask them to share what was listed.

Teacher Notes

_____

_____

_____

_____

_____

_____

STRATEGY: WORD SORTS

Why Use the Word Sorts Strategy?

The purpose of the Word Sorts strategy (Gillet & Kita, 1979) is to help students organize words based upon prior knowledge. A Closed Word Sort requires the teacher to predetermine the categories for the words. The Open Word Sort does not have predetermined categories.

Types of Texts: Fiction, Nonfiction, Expository Text

This strategy can be easily modified for most content areas.

Grade Level Adaptability: 3–12

Levels of Bloom's Taxonomy: Remember, Understand, Apply, Analyze, Evaluate

Steps in the Process

1. Select vocabulary words from selected reading.
2. Write the words on notecards, whiteboard, or overhead transparency.
3. Place students into groups of two to four, and explain that they are to sort words according to pre-established categories (Closed Word Sort).
4. Place students into groups of two to four and explain that they are to review words and group them according to a category they believe appropriate (Open Word Sort).
5. After groups have completed the activity, ask them to share their ideas with the whole class.

Benefits

• Easily implemented

- Requires only moderate advance preparation from the teacher
- Encourages a positive student attitude toward strategy
- Encourages cooperation among classmates
- Helpful in a classroom with students having a wide range of academic ability
- Provides a framework for discussion of vocabulary words
- Facilitates a deeper understanding of the vocabulary words
- Provides for differentiation and teacher flexibility depending upon selected words and use of Closed or Open Word Sort

Considerations

- None noted.

Technology Adaptation

- Project words electronically and ask students to create an electronic display of the categories and words.

Teacher Notes

_____

_____

_____

_____

_____

_____

STRATEGY: WORD STORM

Why Use the Word Storm Strategy?

The Word Storm strategy (Klemp, 1994) was designed to teach vocabulary words and provide opportunity for students to make predictions about how individual words will be used in the context of the selected reading passage.

Types of Texts: Fiction, Nonfiction, Expository Text

This strategy can be easily modified for a variety of content areas.

Grade Level Adaptability: 4–12
Levels of Bloom's Taxonomy: Remember, Understand, Apply, Analyze

Steps in the Process

1. Select key words from a reading passage.
2. Ask students to write the following on a sheet of paper.
   • What is the word?
   • Write the sentence from the text in which the word is used.
   • What are some words you think of when you see the word?
   • Do you know any other forms of the word? If so, what are they?
   • Name three people who would use the word.
   • What are some synonyms for this word?
   • Use the word in a sentence. The sentence should communicate that you understand the definition of the word.
3. After giving students the vocabulary words, ask them to answer the questions and complete the worksheet.

Benefits

• Can be done individually, with a small group, or with the whole class
• Requires only moderate advance preparation from the teacher
• Encourages collaboration of thought
• Provides for differentiation and teacher flexibility depending upon which words are given to specific students
• Applicable for a variety of subjects
• Easy to implement
• Facilitates a deeper understanding of the vocabulary word

Considerations

• If this activity is completed for each vocabulary word, the activity may be too time-consuming.

Technology Adaptation

• Divide students into groups of two to four and provide the passage electronically. Direct them to discuss the sentences and reach consensus as to what the missing word might be. Ask students to type selected words into the electronic passage.
• Display words and questions on computers in a computer lab. Have students rotate around the lab answering one question on each computer.

Teacher Notes

_____

_____

_____

_____

_____

STRATEGY: WORD WEB

Why Use the Word Web Strategy?

The Word Web strategy (Rosenbaum, 2001) is designed to support student vocabulary development by clarifying the definitions of each word while introducing students to related terminology.

Types of Texts: Fiction, Nonfiction, Expository Text

This strategy can be easily modified for a variety of content areas.

Grade Level Adaptability: 3–12

Levels of Bloom's Taxonomy: Remember, Understand, Apply

Steps in the Process

1. Ask students to draw eight oval bubbles on a sheet of paper. Each bubble should be numbered 1 through 8. Bubbles should be in ascending order from the top of the page to the bottom of the page.
2. Direct students to select an unknown word from the selected reading passage and write the word in Bubble 1. Tell students to include the page number from the text where the word is used.
3. In Bubble 2, ask students to record an important sentence from the text that includes the vocabulary word.
4. In Bubble 3, instruct students to use a dictionary or the text glossary and write the definition of the selected word.
5. Ask students to compose their own sentence that includes the vocabulary word. This sentence should further clarify the word meaning. Place the sentence in Bubble 4.
6. Ask students to write a synonym in Bubble 5, an antonym in Bubble 6, and another form of the vocabulary word in Bubble 7.
7. Instruct students to write a phrase, category, or personal clue related to the word in Bubble 8.

Benefits

- Can be done individually, with a small group, or with the whole class
- Requires little advance preparation from the teacher
- Easily implemented
- Provides a deeper understanding of the term
- Facilitates differentiation depending upon words provided to individual students
- Helpful in a classroom with students having a wide range of academic ability
- Requires students to compare and contrast information
- Provides a framework for students to examine words and concepts

Considerations

- This activity may be too time-consuming to do with all vocabulary words.

Technology Adaptation

- Have students create the graphic organizer electronically.

Teacher Notes

_____

_____

_____

_____

_____

STRATEGY: WORDS FOR THE DAY

Why Use the Words for the Day Strategy?

The purpose of the Words for the Day strategy (Rasinski & Padak, 2004) is to encourage students to recognize important vocabulary words and use them orally and in writing during the course of a school day.

Types of Texts: Fiction, Nonfiction, Expository Text

This strategy can be easily modified for a variety of content areas.

Grade Level Adaptability: K–6

Levels of Bloom's Taxonomy: Remember, Understand, Apply

Steps in the Process

1. As new words are introduced throughout the school day, list them on some type of display in the classroom.
2. Encourage students to use the new words during the class period or during the day.
3. As a culminating activity for the lesson, ask students to make a visual representation of the word. If possible, the visual representations should make a personal connection between the student and the vocabulary word.
4. If space permits, keep words posted throughout the week.

Benefits

- Enjoyment of the activity by the students
- Takes little teacher preparation
- Straightforward and easy to explain and understand
- Words can be used as a study guide for a formal assessment
- Provides for differentiation with teacher flexibility and choice of words

Considerations

- There may be a shortage of space to display all the words.

Technology Adaptation

- Post the words on a classroom blog and ask students to continue to use the words, and make connections to them, during the week.
- Ask students to make a listing of all the ways they have used the word during the week and e-mail the list to classmates. The student who records the most legitimate uses for the word during the week wins.

Teacher Notes

Chapter 2

Comprehension Strategies

According to the Longman Dictionary of American English (2004), reading is defined as "the activity of looking at and understanding written words." From the teaching perspective, the emphasis should be on the word *understanding*. Without understanding, there is no *reading*.

If students are to be successful in the schools of the twenty-first century, they must be able to remember and understand what they read. For some, this may be a struggle beginning with instruction at the elementary level. For others, the difficulty may become more apparent when the emphasis evolves from *learning to read* to *reading to learn*. Nonfiction or technical textbooks are challenging.

The strategies in this chapter will be beneficial to most students. Each is designed to encourage the remembering and understanding of difficult text. Some activities will stretch students to the highest levels of Bloom's Taxonomy, while others may require less cognitive effort. Regardless, all require thoughtful consideration from the student, resulting in a greater understanding of content material.

Most of the strategies are explained as first described in the original research. However, a few of the procedures have been modified as a result of feedback from teachers, students, or author experience.

Each strategy has been reviewed related to Bloom's Taxonomy; many have the potential to require higher-order thinking skills. The level of thinking required by students will depend upon how the teacher facilitates questioning. If the purpose of the activity is to encourage application, analysis, or evaluation, teacher questions must be constructed in such a manner as to encourage deep and reflective thought.

STRATEGY: AGREE OR DISAGREE

Why Use the Agree or Disagree Strategy?

The purpose of the Agree or Disagree strategy (Rasinski & Padak, 1996) is to provide a framework for students to use when sharing their thoughts about multi-faceted issues. This technique encourages critical and complex thinking.

Types of Texts: Fiction, Nonfiction, Expository Text

This strategy can be easily modified for a variety of content areas.

Grade Level Adaptability: Grades 4–12

Levels of Bloom's Taxonomy: Remember, Understand, Apply, Analyze, Evaluate

Steps in the Process

1. Formulate several questions related to the reading that reflect varying points of view.
2. Provide questions to the students.
3. After students have read or listened to the selected reading, ask them to write whether they agree or disagree with each statement. Their written statements should include an explanation of why they believe as they do about the topic.
4. After statements are written, discuss with students how to conduct themselves during a discussion that will include a variety of viewpoints. This would include such things as only one person speaking at a time, participants remaining respectful, all being allowed to speak and share opinions, and so forth.
5. Divide students into groups of three to four, directing group members to discuss each statement and decide whether they agree or disagree. One group member should take notes during the discussion and serve as recorder. These notes should include the reasoning behind the opinions expressed by individuals and/or the group.
6. When the small groups have completed their assignment, facilitate a discussion of the statements with the whole class.
7. When discussions are complete, ask students to get into groups based upon their preferred opinions.
8. Compare the groups and discuss whether opinions changed as a result of the reading or class discussion.

Benefits

- Provides a framework for students when reading difficult and challenging material

- Provides teacher flexibility and the opportunity to differentiate instruction depending upon the content of the questions given to each group
- Facilitates a deeper understanding of the text
- Actively engages students in the process of reading and deliberation
- Encourages students to see more than one side of an issue
- Facilitates better preparation for reading expository material as an independent reader
- Provides a constructive opportunity for "arguing" and defending a variety of points of view
- Provides a framework for a civil and respectful discussion
- Facilitates retention through in-depth discussion

Considerations

- Students may be tempted to become too emotional defending a point of view.
- Teacher preparation time is needed to formulate engaging and thought-provoking questions and statements.
- Teachers may need to spend preparatory time explaining the appropriate way to discuss a variety of perspectives in a civil manner.
- Not all text material provides a variety of reader perspectives.
- Teachers will need strong classroom management skills.

Technology Adaptation

- Ask students to explore alternative positions by researching the topic on the Internet. Students should be prepared to agree or disagree with new information and should be prepared to explain what changed their opinions.
- E-mail statements to students and ask them to respond electronically.

Teacher Notes

_____

_____

_____

_____

_____

_____

STRATEGY: ARGUMENTS ON A CARD

Why Use the Arguments on a Card Strategy?

The primary purpose of the Arguments on a Card strategy (Steele, Meridith, & Temple, 1998) is to provide students the opportunity to explore a controversial topic while differentiating points of view and formulating opinions based upon relevant information. This strategy promotes engagement and encourages critical and complex thinking.

Types of Texts: Fiction, Nonfiction, Expository Text

This strategy can be easily modified for a variety of content areas.

Grade Level Adaptability: Grades 5–12

Levels of Bloom's Taxonomy: Remember, Understand, Apply, Analyze, Evaluate

Steps in the Process

1. Introduce a controversial issue or topic to the class.
2. Ask a binary question (yes/no, pro/con).
3. Divide the class into two heterogeneous groups and assign each group a "side" to support or defend.
4. Assign each group relevant reading material. Each group can read different information; however, if the text provides support for both positions, both groups may read the same material.
5. Tell students that their purpose for reading is to support an argument and prepare for a debate with another group.
6. Provide notecards to students for the purpose of recording information supporting their positions.
7. Encourage students to record as many "arguments" as possible. Students may want to work individually or with a partner.
8. After a designated period of time, ask students to bring their cards to a meeting of the larger group for the purpose of sharing all "arguments." Ask each student to share a different idea.
9. Direct groups to decide which arguments are most persuasive and to be prepared to share those arguments with the other half of the class (those representing the opposing view). At this point, each group should plan an opening statement and appoint a person to make the statement to the class.
10. After each side has made the opening statement, individuals should offer reasons and support for their position.
11. Encourage students to argue a position with which they do not initially agree.

Benefits

- Controversial topics are usually of high interest to students
- Actively engages students in the purpose for reading—to frame an "argument"
- Facilitates critical thinking
- Provides a specific purpose for reading the text
- Supports retention of information through purposeful discussion of topic
- Provides a constructive opportunity for "arguing" and defending a variety of points of view
- Provides a framework for a civil and respectful discussion
- Applicable for a variety of subjects

Considerations

- Students may be tempted to become too emotional defending a point of view.
- Teacher preparation time is needed to consider controversial texts and locate adequate information supporting more than one point of view.
- Teachers will need strong classroom management skills.
- Not all curriculum content provides a variety of reader perspectives.

Technology Adaptation

- Rather than notecards, ask students to produce an electronic PowerPoint presentation including critical issues and perspectives. The grading rubric for the assignment could include creativity and novelty of presentation.
- Ask students to explore the topic on the Internet and create a PowerPoint explaining their opinions and stated positions.

Teacher Notes

_____

_____

_____

_____

_____

_____

_____

STRATEGY: ASKED AND ANSWERED

Why Use the Asked and Answered Strategy?

The purpose of the Asked and Answered strategy is to help students develop the ability to ask questions and read for deeper meaning. It provides students the opportunity to both formulate and answer comprehension questions.

Types of Texts: Fiction, Nonfiction, Expository Text

This strategy can be easily modified for a variety of content areas.

Grade Level Adaptability: Grades 5–12

Levels of Bloom's Taxonomy: Remember, Understand, Apply, Analyze, Evaluate

Steps in the Process

1. Provide each student with three to five index cards.
2. Ask students to read the text and write three to five questions (one question per card). Encourage students to ask questions that require application, analysis, or evaluation of the text.
3. Place students into groups of two and ask them to trade cards.
4. Direct each student to read the respective cards and write possible answers on the back of the card.
5. After possible answers have been recorded, ask students to discuss their answers and the topic further.
6. Ask each pair of students to create additional questions and record them on new index cards.
7. Instruct each pair of students to work with another pair of students and discuss the questions that have been generated.
8. This process can be repeated until there is a group of six students.

Benefits

- Actively engages students in the discussion of reading content
- Provides a specific purpose for reading the text
- Purposeful discussion of topic supports retention of information
- Applicable for a variety of subjects
- Differentiates depending upon choice of questions generated
- Straightforward and easy to explain
- Takes little teacher preparation
- Allows for both small- and large-group discussion
- Easy to implement

Considerations

- Classroom management skills need to be evident.
- Sample content questions may need to be provided to students.
- The teacher will need to monitor each group closely to ensure appropriate participation.

Technology Adaptation

- Create a classroom blog that allows students to respond electronically to questions and ideas.
- Rather than using notecards, use a computer lab and display one comprehension question on each computer. Ask students to rotate around the room answering questions and making comments related to the topic.

Teacher Notes

_____

_____

_____

_____

_____

_____

STRATEGY: ATTRIBUTE WEB

Why Use the Attribute Web Strategy?

The purpose of the Attribute Web strategy (Lenski, Wham, Johns, & Caskey, 2007) is to provide students the opportunity to analyze a character from a text and construct a visual representation of that individual. This activity provides students the opportunity to visualize how a character looks, acts, or feels. The Attribute Web may also include how other characters within the text perceive the individual.

Types of Texts: Fiction, Nonfiction, Expository Text

This strategy can be easily modified for a variety of content areas.

Grade Level Adaptability: K–12

Levels of Bloom's Taxonomy: Remember, Understand, Apply, Analyze, Evaluate

Steps in the Process

1. Discuss the importance of character analysis, including a review of the attributes of a character within the reading. Attributes may include physical characteristics or personality characteristics, or a combination of the two.
2. After reading the selection, ask students to work individually or in small groups to create the Attribute Web.
3. Instruct students to draw a circle in the middle of a piece of paper and place the character's name in the circle.
4. Using the basic web format, ask students to brainstorm what they consider to be significant attributes of the character and include the listing on the web. The attributes may include single words or descriptive phrases.
5. Ask students to share the web with others.

Benefits

- Provides opportunity for individual work or a collaborative effort
- Encourages attention to detail and student engagement
- Takes little teacher preparation
- Straightforward and easy to explain and understand
- Helps students understand how an author develops a storyline through characterization
- Encourages collaboration
- Provides a purpose for reading
- Good activity for a substitute teacher
- May be an ongoing activity while book is being read

Considerations

- None noted.

Technology Adaptation

- Use one of the free word web frameworks available on the Internet. Ask students to select an organizer and create an electronic Attribute Web using sound, color, and animation.

Teacher Notes

_____

_____

STRATEGY: AUTHOR'S CHAIR

Why Use the Author's Chair Strategy?

The purpose of the Author's Chair strategy (Graves & Hansen, 1983) is to provide an opportunity for students to present their writing to peers and evaluate the writing of classmates through the use of constructive feedback.

Types of Texts: Fiction, Nonfiction, Expository Text

This strategy can be easily modified for most content areas.

Grade Level Adaptability: Grades 2–9

Levels of Bloom's Taxonomy: Remember, Understand, Apply, Analyze, Evaluate

Steps in the Process

1. Provide students with reading material and questions related to the topic.
2. Tell students to use the questions as a guide for a written response to the reading.
3. Explain that each student will share his writing with the class while sitting in the Author's Chair. This can be a specific chair in the front of the room, or each student's individual chair can become the Author's Chair.
4. After completion of the writing project, each student presents individual writing to the class.
5. Instruct the audience to make notes and share comments about the writing with the author. Comments may be related to accuracy of content, writing style, interpretation of content, suggestions for improvement, and so forth.

Benefits

- Supports student accountability since all will be responsible for a class presentation
- Encourages interdependence and civility within the classroom
- Applicable for a variety of subjects
- Supports retention of material and development of writing skills

- Facilitates listening skills
- Good activity for a substitute teacher
- Encourages critical thinking

Considerations

- The teacher will need to monitor student participation to ensure that all take part in the discussion.
- Teacher preparation time is needed to formulate engaging and multi-faceted questions.
- The teacher may need to spend preparatory time explaining to students the appropriate way to provide constructive feedback.
- This lesson is time-consuming in terms of student presentations.
- Some students will need to practice with the teacher prior to a class presentation.

Technology Adaptation

- Have an "Author Chair" on a class website. Encourage students to share their writing with others electronically.
- Use an electronic rubric to provide feedback to students.

Teacher Notes

_____

_____

_____

_____

_____

STRATEGY: CHARACTER QUOTES

Why Use the Character Quotes Strategy?

The purpose of the Character Quotes strategy (Buehl, 2001) is to motivate students to read the assigned text, as well as to help them analyze and predict character traits of an individual in the upcoming reading selection. This activity is an engaging "set" to a lesson when students are expected to read about an individual.

Types of Texts: Fiction, Nonfiction, Expository Text

This strategy can be easily modified for a variety of content areas. It is especially effective with biographies, autobiographies, and any other text that includes quotations from a historical figure.

Grade Level Adaptability: 4–12

Levels of Bloom's Taxonomy: Remember, Understand, Apply, Analyze, Evaluate

Steps in the Process

1. Preview the text for the purpose of finding quotes from a character that provide insight into the individual's personality.
2. All quotes should be from the same character within the text.
3. Write quotes on individual pieces of paper for distribution to student groups.
4. Divide students into groups of three to four and give each group one to three quotes.
5. Tell students all quotes are from the same character.
6. Instruct students to make predictions based on the quotations related to the personality of the character. Encourage them to generate as many words or descriptors as possible.
7. When all groups have completed the assignment, ask one individual from each group to read the quotation and descriptors to the class. For the purpose of comparison, these traits should be recorded on a transparency or marker board.
8. Encourage discussion as to what was stated in the quotation that gave clues or hints related to personality traits.
9. Tell students to read the text for the purpose of determining whether predictions were accurate.
10. If time allows, ask students to write a personality profile of the character. Tell them they may be asked to read the profile to the class.

Benefits

- Enhances reading by making predictions
- Provides positive interaction with peers
- Activates background knowledge
- Facilitates a deeper understanding of the text, as well as a character within the text
- Engages all students in a classroom with students having a wide range of academic ability

- Provides differentiation through the choice of selected quotations for each group
- Allows for both small-group and large-group discussion
- Encourages critical thinking

Considerations

- Initial teacher preparation may take time due to the importance of locating insightful and appropriate character quotations.

Technology Adaptation

- After students know the name of the character or individual, ask them to use the Internet to locate information related to how others might have described the individual. Have students compare or contrast different perspectives.
- Use a computer lab and display a different quote on each computer. Have students move around the room and list character traits related to the displayed quote. After students have rotated through the room, assign each student to a computer and have him or her read the quote and what was recorded to the class.

Teacher Notes

_____

_____

_____

_____

_____

STRATEGY: CONVERSATIONAL DISCUSSION GROUPS

Why Use the Conversational Discussion Group Strategy?

The primary purpose of the Conversational Discussion Group strategy (Tierney & Readance, 2000) is to create and facilitate an environment where students explore and construct meaning from a passage and then share ideas with others.

Types of Texts: Fiction, Nonfiction, Expository Text
This strategy can be easily modified for most content areas.
Grade Level Adaptability: 6–12
Levels of Bloom's Taxonomy: Remember, Understand, Apply, Analyze, Evaluate

Steps in the Process

1. Designate heterogeneous groups of four to six students.
2. Explain the rules of the lesson. It might be helpful to leave the rules for the lesson posted where students and teacher can reference them during the activity:
   a. Speak one at a time, and stay on subject.
   b. If you say yes or no, state why.
   c. Ask questions when discussion is quiet.
   d. Participate.
   e. Shared ideas can be supported by information from the text or by personal experience.
3. Present the first question to student groups. It is helpful to have each question projected or written where students can see it as they participate in the discussion. The first question should be open-ended, and designed to activate student background knowledge. As students are provided a discussion question, explain how much time will be provided for the discussion.
4. After a designated period of time, provide students written text, and instruct them to read silently for the purpose of remembering as much as possible.
5. After students have been provided sufficient time for reading, present another question for discussion. The second question should be one that stimulates dialogue at the lower levels of Bloom's Taxonomy (Remember or Understand).
6. When the discussion of the second question is completed, give students the third question. This question should be at a higher level on Bloom's Taxonomy and should require students to think beyond the text (Apply, Analyze, or Evaluate).
7. At the completion of the discussion of the third question, facilitate a whole-class discussion of the reading material.

Benefits

- Encourages students to actively participate in the lesson
- Encourages critical thinking

- Facilitates a deeper understanding of the text
- Good activity for a class having a wide range of reading ability
- Encourages interdependence within the classroom and the individual groups
- Applicable for a variety of subjects
- Easy to implement
- Supports retention of material
- Encourages a positive student attitude toward strategy

Considerations

- The teacher should monitor each group closely to ensure that all students participate equally in the discussion.
- Teacher preparation time is needed to formulate questions and statements that are engaging and multi-faceted.
- Preparation time may be necessary to explain the appropriate way of discussing a variety of perspectives in a civil manner.

Technology Adaptation

- After students are provided the third question, ask them to use the Internet to research the topic for additional information.

Teacher Notes

STRATEGY: CORNELL NOTE-TAKING

Why Use Cornell Note-Taking Strategy?

The primary purpose of the Cornell Note-Taking strategy (Pauk, 1974) is to provide students an organized and efficient method of taking lecture notes or notes from a text. This note-taking system provides an easy-to-use study guide.

Types of Texts: Nonfiction, Expository Text
This strategy can be easily modified for most content areas.
Grade Level Adaptability: 6–12
Levels of Bloom's Taxonomy: Remember, Understand

Steps in the Process

1. Tell students to draw a line vertically on the left side of a piece of paper.
2. Instruct them to write important information from the lecture or text in the column on the right side of the paper.
3. After notes are completed, tell students to review the notes and write questions from the content in the margin on the left.
4. Ask students to cover the right column, exposing only the questions on the left. Students should self-quiz or work within a small group of students to learn the important concepts.

Benefits

- Promotes active listening
- Provides a systematic method for note-taking
- Provides a ready-made study guide for review
- Easy to implement
- Supports retention of material

Considerations

- Some students may resist if they have already developed their own method for taking notes.

Technology Adaptation

- Have students record notes electronically.

Teacher Notes

_____

_____

_____

_____

STRATEGY:
DIRECTED READING THINKING ACTIVITY (DRTA)

Why Use the Directed Reading Thinking Activity Strategy?

The purpose of the Directed Reading Thinking Activity strategy (Stauffer, 1976) is to help students read critically and reflect upon what they read. This strategy helps students determine a purpose for reading, carefully examine the text, and remain engaged throughout the lesson. Although this strategy can be modified for nonfiction (Content Directed Thinking Activity), it is easily implemented with fiction.

The teacher uses three basic questions. What do you think is going to happen? Why do you think so? Can you prove it?

Types of Texts: Fiction, Nonfiction, Expository Text

This strategy can be easily modified for most content areas.

Grade Level Adaptability: K–12 (With primary grades, this could be a listening activity.)

Levels of Bloom's Taxonomy: Remember, Understand, Apply, Analyze

Steps in the Process

1. Read the selection to select predetermined stopping points.
2. Tell students they will need a cover sheet.
3. Ask students to cover everything but the title of the selection.
4. Tell students to read the title and make predictions about the story contents.
5. As students make predictions, ask for "evidence" supporting their belief that their predictions are correct.
6. Ask students to read a portion of the text up to a predetermined stopping point. Tell them that they will review their initial predictions, as well as make new predictions based upon the reading. Students should use paper to cover text that has not yet been read.
7. After students have finished reading the designated text, ask questions.

Fiction: What has happened so far? What do you think is going to happen next? Why do you think so? Can you prove it; or, why do you think so?

Nonfiction: What do you need to remember about what you read? What do you think the author will discuss in the next section? Why do you think so? What do you consider to be most important from the reading?

Continue the process until text selection has been read completely.

Benefits

- Easily implemented
- Requires active participation from the reader
- Requires only moderate advance preparation from the teacher
- Good activity for substitute teachers
- Encourages a positive student attitude toward strategy
- Encourages silent reading
- Helpful in classroom when students have a wide range of academic ability
- Teachers "think aloud" with students as predictions and answers are formulated
- Works one on one, with small groups, and with the whole class
- Breaks the passage into manageable parts for students and teacher
- Can easily be implemented with nonfiction text

Considerations

- This strategy may slow the reading of advanced readers.

Technology Adaptation

None noted.

Teacher Notes

_____

_____

_____

_____

STRATEGY: FOCUSED FREE WRITES

Why Use the Focused Free Writes Strategy?

The primary purpose of the Focused Free Writes strategy (Unrau, 2004) is to assist students in clarifying and organizing ideas and thoughts related to a specific topic or reading passage. This strategy provides structure and choice for students.

Types of Texts: Fiction, Nonfiction, Expository Text
This strategy can be easily modified for a variety of content areas.
Grade Level Adaptability: 4–12
Levels of Bloom's Taxonomy: Remember, Understand, Apply, Analyze, Evaluate

Steps in the Process

1. Activate students' background knowledge related to the topic.
2. Explain to students that they will be asked to respond in writing to a question or statement provided by the teacher after completing the reading.
3. Provide question and written text to students.
4. When students have finished reading the text, the teacher should provide the question, allowing three to five minutes for them to write a response. More time may be allowed for writing if the question requires a deeper understanding of the text.
5. Encourage students to use vocabulary words from the reading in their reflections.
6. After students have completed the writing assignment, ask for volunteers to share written responses with the class. A variation would be to ask students to share their responses within smaller groups.
7. Students may come to front of the room and sit in an "Author Chair" while they read.
8. Prepare a free write to use as an example if you sense students need modeling of the product.

Benefits

- Requires reflection and written response
- Provides teacher flexibility with content of the questions
- Provides for differentiation among students
- Facilitates a deeper understanding of the text
- Actively engages readers in the reading process by setting a specific purpose for the reading
- Provides for individualized instruction, as well as the opportunity for collaboration

Considerations

- Some students may benefit from having the questions in advance to assist in recognition of important versus unimportant information.

Technology Adaptation

• Ask students to use a classroom blog to post their written assignments.

Teacher Notes

_____

_____

_____

_____

STRATEGY: GALLERY TOUR

Why Use the Gallery Tour Strategy?

The purpose of the Gallery Tour strategy (Rasinski & Padak, 1996) is to have students produce a visual display of the content of a text or other information learned during the unit of instruction. The strategy also allows other students to view the visual interpretation of classmates while offering suggestions for improvement of the visual representation.

Types of Texts: Fiction, Nonfiction, Expository Text

This strategy can be easily modified for a variety of content areas.

Grade Level Adaptability: 6–12

Levels of Bloom's Taxonomy: Remember, Understand, Apply, Analyze, Evaluate

Steps in the Process

1. Explain to students that they will be working with a small group of class-mates to produce a product such as a diagram or map of the information on a piece of chart paper. If this is the first time for the activity, further explanation of product types may be necessary.
2. Provide selection for students to read.
3. When students have finished reading, ask them to work individually or in groups of three to four for the purpose of creating a visual representation of the content. The drawing can include words or symbols, or a combination of both.
4. After completion of the visual representation, tape the products around the room and display them on the walls.

5. Provide each student with small pieces of notepaper to place on the wall around the projects. This will be used to provide feedback related to the critique of the product.
6. Tell students to walk around the room as individuals, or with a small group, and to critique each visual representation while posting comments.
7. Instruct each student to provide a minimum of one original comment to each display.
8. After the tour, ask groups to review the notes and reexamine the representation in comparison to others.

Benefits

- Takes little teacher preparation
- Straightforward, easy to explain and understand
- Novel way of displaying information from the text
- Actively engages students with a wide variety of reading ability
- Encourages visual imaging of reading content
- Requires evaluative thought related to the work of others

Considerations

- If visual displays are not thought-provoking or accurate, the tour may be unproductive and frustrating for teacher and students.

Technology Adaptation

- Ask students to design an electronic, pictorial collage to post for the Gallery Tour.
- Tell students to e-mail the electronic collage to classmates and ask for constructive feedback. Provide feedback electronically.

Teacher Notes

_____

_____

_____

_____

_____

STRATEGY: GROUP MAPPING

Why Use the Group Mapping Strategy?

The purpose of the Group Mapping strategy (Davidson, 1982) is to help students remember detail as well as summarize the main idea from the manuscript. Maps can be done individually or with small groups of students. While designing the visual representation of the content, students are encouraged to discuss the reading with classmates. Students can use nonlinguistic representations, words, or a combination of words and symbols to complete the map.

Types of Texts: Fiction, Nonfiction, Expository Text

This strategy can be easily modified for most content areas.

Grade Level Adaptability: 5–12

Levels of Bloom's Taxonomy: Remember, Understand, Apply

Steps in the Process

1. Activate the students' prior knowledge of the topic.
2. Tell students the purpose for reading is to create a representation of the information. Representations can include the main idea, as well as more detailed information. If the product is to be displayed or shared with others, students should understand that this is part of the assignment.
3. Students read the text.
4. After completion of the reading, tell students to work individually or with a small group to create a visual representation of the text. Student groups should remain small to ensure active participation from everyone. If the visual image is to be shared with the class or displayed in some manner, large paper should be used.
5. When each group has completed the task, ask students to display each map and be ready to provide an explanation of its content to the whole class.

Benefits

- Easily implemented
- Requires only moderate advance preparation from the teacher
- Encourages a positive student attitude toward strategy
- Encourages cooperation among classmates
- Helpful in classroom having students with a wide range of academic ability
- Provides a framework for discussion of text
- Can easily be implemented with nonfiction text
- Facilitates a deeper understanding of the text
- Encourages visual imagery

Considerations

• The teachers will need to monitor each group ensuring that all participate equally in the discussion and creation of the visual display.

Technology Adaptation

• Ask students to design an electronic collage using symbols, pictures, or words.
• Direct students to e-mail the electronic collage to classmates and ask for constructive feedback. Provide feedback electronically.

Teacher Notes

_____

_____

_____

_____

_____

STRATEGY: INSTRUCTIONAL CLOZE

Why Use the Instructional Cloze Strategy?

The Instructional Cloze strategy (Lenski, Wham, Johns, & Caskey, 2007) was designed to facilitate the use of context clues to predict text and vocabulary words. It provides an opportunity for students and teacher to think out loud about the use of contextual analysis.

Types of Texts: Fiction, Nonfiction, Expository Text

This strategy can be easily modified for a variety of content areas.

Grade Level Adaptability: 1–6

Levels of Bloom's Taxonomy: Remember, Understand, Apply

Steps in the Process

1. Select a reading passage.
2. Retype the passage keeping the first and last sentence in tact. Beginning with the second sentence, delete every fifth word and replace it with a blank space. All blank spaces should be of equal length.

3. Number the blanks.
4. Project the sentences on a screen for student viewing. If a projector is not available, provide each student a paper with the passage printed.
5. Explain that the purpose of the activity is to help understand the importance of using context clues, sentence length, and background knowledge when reading and understanding a text.
6. Working individually, in small groups, or as a whole class, ask students to predict the exact wording for each blank space, explaining why they chose a specific word by answering questions such as, "Why did you choose that particular word?" "How did you decide upon that specific word?" and "What other words did you consider?'

Benefits

- Can be done individually, with a small group, or with the whole class
- Requires only moderate advance preparation from the teacher
- Encourages collaboration of thought
- Helpful in classroom having students with a wide range of academic ability
- Requires understanding and analyzing
- Teaches a skill that good readers must possess
- Applicable for a variety of subjects
- Encourages critical thinking

Considerations

- This strategy may not be necessary for more advanced students.

Technology Adaptation

- Divide students into groups of three to four, and provide the passage electronically. Direct them to discuss the sentences and reach consensus on the choice of word. The selected word can then be typed into the electronic passage.

Teacher Notes

_____

_____

_____

_____

_____

STRATEGY: KNOW, WANT, AND LEARN (KWL)

Why Use the Know, Want, and Learn Strategy?

The purpose of the Know, Want, and Learn strategy (Ogle, 1986) is to actively engage students before, during, and after reading a text. This strategy facilitates activation of background knowledge and provides important information to the teacher about what students know or don't know about the topic to be studied. This strategy also helps students organize their thoughts prior to reading, provides a structure for student predictions related to the reading, and presents a purpose for completing the reading task—that is, to answer the questions from the middle column.

Types of Texts: Fiction, Nonfiction, Expository Text
This strategy can be easily modified for a variety of content areas.

Grade Level Adaptability: K–12 (With primary students this may need to be a listening, rather than a reading, activity.)

Levels of Bloom's Taxonomy: Remember, Understand, Apply, Analyze

Steps in the Process

1. Provide students with the topic of the unit or reading selection.
2. Ask students to divide a piece of paper into three columns of equal size. The teacher may draw a similar graphic organizer on a marker board.
3. Above the column on the left, ask students to write the word "KNOW." Above the middle column, direct students to write the word "WANT," and under the right column, ask students to write the word "LEARN."
4. Explain to students that before they begin reading on a specific topic, they should always reflect upon what they already know. Have students brainstorm and record what they already "KNOW" about the subject and place the information in the appropriate column. If students provide incorrect facts, record them and make corrections after the reading. Teacher records information on the marker board, and students record information on individual papers.
5. Tell students to brainstorm what they "WANT" to know about the topic and place questions in the middle column. Be prepared to supply questions if students seem unsure of what to ask.
6. Instruct students to read the text for the purpose of answering the questions, as well as to correct any misinformation previously recorded.
7. After the reading is completed, have students discuss and complete the third column on the right side of the paper. If possible, this should include writing answers to the questions from the middle column, as well as other pertinent information gleaned from the text.

Benefits

- Provides a structure and purpose for reading
- Activates background knowledge of students
- Provides critical information for teacher about students' preconceived knowledge
- Takes little teacher preparation
- Straightforward, easy to explain and understand
- Helpful tool for students to use when reading independently
- Can be done individually, in a small group, or with the whole class
- Good activity for a substitute teacher

Considerations

- It may be a difficult activity to facilitate if students have little prior knowledge of topic.
- Strong readers may receive limited benefit from this activity.

Technology Adaptation

- Ask students to work individually or with a small group to display an electronic graphic organizer using the KWL format. Ask students to present the finished products to the whole class.

Teacher Notes

_____

_____

_____

_____

_____

STRATEGY: KNOWLEDGE CHART

Why Use the Knowledge Chart Strategy?

The Knowledge Chart strategy (Marzano, 2004) was designed to encourage students to think about what they already know and relate it to what they read from the text. This strategy supports student understanding of the main idea, as well as detailed information, from the text.

Types of Texts: Fiction, Nonfiction, Expository Text

This strategy can be easily modified for a variety of content areas.
Grade Level Adaptability: 3–12
Levels of Bloom's Taxonomy: Remember, Understand

Steps in the Process

1. Locate a text or visual images to share with students.
2. Give students paper and ask them to divide it vertically into two columns of equal size. The teacher may draw a similar graphic organizer on a marker board.
3. At the top of the column on the left, ask students to write "Prior Knowledge." At the top of the column on the right, ask them to write "New Knowledge."
4. Prior to reading the assigned text, ask students to brainstorm what they already know about the topic and record the information in the column under "Prior Knowledge."
5. After reading the passage, have students list in the "New Knowledge" column information from what they have read. Students should continue until they have listed several pieces of new information.
6. Using the information from both columns, ask students to work individually or in small groups to formulate questions for what they would still like to learn about the topic.

Benefits

- Can be done individually, with a small group, or with the whole class
- Requires moderate advance preparation from the teacher
- Novel method of activating background knowledge
- Sets a specific purpose for reading
- Helpful in classroom with students having a wide range of academic ability
- Requires students to compare and contrast information
- Good activity for a substitute teacher
- Serves as a study guide

Considerations

- If students lack initial background knowledge of the topic, additional discussion will need to occur prior to having them read the text.

Technology Adaptation

- Tell students to research the topic on the Internet as a pre-reading or post-reading activity. Ask them to record the information on the Knowledge Chart.

- Ask students to create the Knowledge Chart electronically using pictures, words, or symbols.

Teacher Notes

_____

_____

_____

_____

_____

STRATEGY: LITERATURE CIRCLES

Why Use the Literature Circles Strategy?

The purpose of the Literature Circles strategy (Daniels, 1994) is to facilitate student-led discussions related to self-selected reading material. This strategy supports comprehension at all levels of Bloom's Taxonomy.

Types of Texts: Fiction, Nonfiction, Expository Text

Grade Level Adaptability: 7–12

Levels of Bloom's Taxonomy: Remember, Understand, Apply, Analyze, Evaluate

Steps in the Process

1. Direct students to choose their own reading selection. It is helpful to designate a genre or several books from which to chose.
2. Assign student groups based upon chosen reading material.
3. Encourage students to use sticky notes, highlighting, or other forms of note-taking.
4. Tell students they will be participating in small-group discussions of the reading material at selected points within the lesson.
5. After students have read up to an agreed-upon chapter in the book, provide class time for discussion of the reading material. Encourage students to make personal connections to the material. As a variation of the strategy, provide sample questions for student consideration. These questions can be provided as a pre-reading or post-reading part of the strategy.
6. Explain that all students are to participate equally during the discussion.
7. The extent of the teacher's role in the group is a professional decision made by the instructor.

Sample discussion questions may include:

How did you feel about _____?

What if _____?

What do you think will happen after _____?

Summarize what happened when _____?

How did the character feel when _____?

How is this book different from others you have read?

How is this book similar to others you have read?

Benefits

- Provides student choice of reading selection
- Encourages student-initiated discussion
- Engages most students
- Encourages active and purposeful learning
- Straightforward, easy to explain and understand
- Provides novelty
- Can be done as a culminating activity or as a review for a more formal assessment
- Differentiation of content based upon selection of reading material and sample discussion questions

Considerations

- The assessment of learning may be challenging.
- The activity may take several class periods to complete.
- Some students may lack personal commitment to the activity.
- Teacher preparation time may increase due to the need for familiarity of reading selections and planning discussions of several texts simultaneously.

Technology Adaptation

- Ask students to utilize classroom blogs to discuss the book's content.
- As a culminating activity, ask students to create an electronic visual representation of the book to share with the class.

Teacher Notes

_____

_____

_____

_____

_____

STRATEGY: MUSIC TO MY EARS

Why Use the Music to My Ears Strategy?

The purpose of the Music to My Ears strategy is to utilize a novel way of providing closure to a lesson. This strategy facilitates attention to detail and summarization of the designated text. Additionally, it affords students the opportunity to listen to fast-paced music while moving around the room.

Types of Texts: Fiction, Nonfiction, Expository Text

This strategy can be easily modified for a variety of content areas.

Grade Level Adaptability: 6–12

Levels of Bloom's Taxonomy: Remember, Understand

Steps in the Process

1. Provide text for students to read.
2. Tell students that the purpose for reading the selection is to look for what they consider to be important information. Explain that they should be prepared to summarize the reading to classmates.
3. After reading the selection, students should write five to seven ideas or concepts learned from the reading.
4. Tell students they will be moving around the room as the music plays. This works best when the music is relatively fast-paced.
5. When the music stops, tell students to find someone standing in close proximity and explain what they have learned and what they want to remember from the reading.
6. When provided new information from other students about what was most important, ask students to add these ideas to their own personal listing.
7. Instruct students not to speak with any student more than once during the activity.
8. As the music continues, ask students to share information from their own original listing or share something discussed with another student.

Benefits

- Provides a purpose for reading
- Takes little teacher preparation

- Encourages active learning
- Straightforward and easy to explain and understand
- Provides novelty for closure
- Can be done as a culminating activity for a unit or as a review for a more formal assessment
- Enjoyable for students

Considerations

- This activity requires adequate space to move throughout the classroom.
- Classroom management skills must be evident by the teacher.

Technology Adaptation

- Have students recommend musical selection. The music should be fast-paced, with appropriate lyrics.

Teacher Notes

_____

_____

_____

_____

_____

STRATEGY: PLUS, MINUS, INTERESTING

Why Use the Plus, Minus, Interesting Strategy?

The Plus, Minus, Interesting strategy (De Bono, 1994) was designed to help students focus attention to more than one perspective and opinion. This strategy facilitates student analysis of the reading content.

Types of Texts: Fiction, Nonfiction, Expository Text
This strategy can be easily modified for a variety of content areas.
Grade Level Adaptability: 6–12
Levels of Bloom's Taxonomy: Remember, Understand

Steps in the Process

1. Ask students to read or listen to a reading selection or a story.

2. Have students make three vertical columns of equal size on a sheet of paper. They should label the columns "P," "M," and "I."
   a. "P" represents "Plus," or good points within the text or story.
   b. "M" represents "Minus," or points of disagreement.
   c. "I" represents "Interesting" information.
3. Ask students to read the text and make note of information they would include within each column.
4. Challenge students to consider a variety of perspectives.
5. When organizers are complete, ask students to share their respective lists with a partner or with a small group of students.
6. When the sharing is complete, facilitate a discussion of the material with the whole class.

Benefits

- Can be done individually, with a small group, or with the whole class
- Requires moderate advance preparation from the teacher
- Novel method of interacting with text
- Sets a specific purpose for reading
- Helpful in classroom with students having a wide range of academic ability
- Requires students to consider a variety of perspectives
- Good activity for a substitute teacher
- May serve as a guide for further study

Considerations

- Some students may find it difficult to consider a perspective other than their own.

Technology Adaptation

- Tell students to research the topic on the Internet to find further information on the topic. Ask them to record the information on the Plus, Minus, Interesting Chart.
- Ask students to create the Plus, Minus, Interesting Chart electronically using pictures, words, or symbols.

Teacher Notes

STRATEGY: POINT COUNTERPOINT

Why Use the Point Counterpoint Strategy?

The purpose of the Point Counterpoint strategy (Rogers, 1991) is to empower readers with the ability to consider a variety of interpretations of a text or reading. It encourages students to interpret the reading for themselves, as opposed to always deferring to the opinions or interpretations of teachers, texts, and others.

Types of Texts: Fiction, Nonfiction, Expository Text

This strategy can be easily modified for a variety of content areas.

Grade Level Adaptability: Grades 6–12 (This is best done with advanced readers.)

Levels of Bloom's Taxonomy: Remember, Understand, Apply, Analyze, Evaluate

Steps in the Process

1. Activate background knowledge by facilitating discussion related to what students already know about the topic or subject.
2. Instruct students to write ideas or responses to the reading as the text is read. This can include, but need not be limited to, reflections of a personal nature, themes of the story, points of confusion, predictions of further reading, and questions for the author, the teacher, or others.
3. After completing the reading, students should discuss with others what they wrote. This can include a comparison to other ideas or a discussion of how ideas may differ, depending upon interpretation.
4. Provide examples of how others may interpret the reading selection.
5. After discussion within small groups or as a whole class, ask students to reconsider their interpretation and decide upon a final perspective.

Benefits

- Provides structure for students when reading difficult and challenging material
- Provides for differentiation among students
- Facilitates a deeper understanding of the text based upon personal interpretation

- Actively engages readers in the reading process
- Facilitates better preparation for reading material as an independent reader
- Encourages reflection on original ideas, including the ideas of others
- Facilitates critical thinking

Considerations

- This strategy may be too difficult for readers who need a great deal of teacher support.
- If there is a lack of student background knowledge of the topic, the strategy may be unproductive.
- Some students may resist when required to "think" rather than to write a rote response.

Technology Adaptation

- Ask students to research both points of view on the Internet and to be prepared to share additional thoughts and perspectives.

Teacher Notes

_____

_____

_____

_____

_____

_____

STRATEGY: PREREADING PLAN (PREP)

Why Use the Prereading Strategy?

The purpose of the Prereading Plan strategy (Langer, 1981) is to facilitate student interest in an upcoming reading assignment, as well as to pre-assess the student background knowledge of the topic.

Types of Texts: Fiction, Nonfiction, Expository Text

This strategy can be easily modified for a variety of content areas.

Grade Level Adaptability: 4–12

Levels of Bloom's Taxonomy: Remember, Understand, Apply, Analyze

Steps in the Process

1. Select important terms from the reading. These should be words students must understand if they are to comprehend the text.
2. Identify the central concept and introduce the topic to the students, explaining that they need to think about what they already know about the topic before they begin to read.
3. Divide students into groups of three to four, and ask them to list ideas that come to mind when they think of the subject.
4. Ask groups to share their lists with the whole class.
5. As students share ideas, record the lists and display them to the class.
6. After all ideas have been listed, ask students to organize the words into a format that makes sense to them. This can include categorizing words with labels or putting the words into some type of graphic organizer.
7. When group displays are complete, ask students to share ideas with the whole class.

Benefits

- Straightforward, easy to explain and understand
- Good activity for a substitute teacher
- Novel way of activating background knowledge
- Facilitates a deeper understanding of the text based upon personal interpretation
- Facilitates better preparation for reading material as an independent reader
- Encourages collaboration
- Facilitates critical thinking

Considerations

- Teacher modeling a graphic organizer may help some students get started with the activity.

Technology Adaptation

- Display the terms and lists electronically.

Teacher Notes

_____

_____

_____

STRATEGY: PREVIEW, QUESTION, READ, REFLECT, RECITE, AND REVIEW (PQ4)

Why Use the Preview, Question, Read, Reflect, Recite, and Review Strategy?

The purpose of the Preview, Question, Read, Reflect, Recite, and Review strategy (Slavin, 1994) is to provide students with a structure for reading difficult and challenging text. This strategy includes activation of prior knowledge through surveying text, as well as questioning and setting a purpose for reading.

Types of Texts: Nonfiction, Expository Text
This strategy can be easily modified for a variety of content areas.
Grade Level Adaptability: Grades 6–12
Levels of Bloom's Taxonomy: Remember, Understand, Apply, Analyze

Steps in the Process

1. Ask students to preview the text by looking at the title, subtitles, visual aids, graphics, headings, and subheadings. While previewing, ask them to consider what they already know about the topic.
2. Instruct students to formulate questions by turning the subheadings into questions. Questions should be recorded on paper.
3. Tell students that their purpose for reading is to answer the written questions.
4. After questions are answered, have students reflect or discuss questions with others. Encourage students to compare questions with others.
5. Ask students to speak their answers to questions aloud. Explain that this will help put the information into their long-term memory.
6. As a closing activity, ask students to review the text and all questions with answers.

Benefits

- Provides structure for students when reading difficult and challenging material
- Gives a specific purpose for reading
- Facilitates a deeper understanding of the text based upon interpretation

- Actively engages readers in the reading process
- Easily done by reader when a teacher is not present
- Provides for reading, recitation, and written work

Considerations

- Some students may resist this activity due to a perception of time commitment.
- Some students may have difficulty formulating thought-provoking questions.

Technology Adaptation

- Ask students to prepare questions with answers electronically and to share the questions and answers with the whole class.

Teacher Notes

_____

_____

_____

_____

STRATEGY: QUESTION, REDUCE, READ, AND REVIEW

Why Use the Question, Reduce, Read, and Review Strategy?

The purpose of the Question, Reduce, Read, and Review strategy is to provide a comprehensive way for students and teachers to engage with text. It provides activation of background knowledge, outlining or graphic organization, and reader reflection. This strategy is particularly beneficial to students when the reading is difficult and complex.

Types of Texts: Fiction, Nonfiction, Expository Text
This strategy can be easily modified for a variety of content areas.
Grade Level Adaptability: 3–12
Levels of Bloom's Taxonomy: Remember, Understand

Steps in the Process

1. Ask students to brainstorm what they already know about the topic.
2. Provide a graphic organizer or outline of the information, and discuss the contents with the class. This can be provided on paper or electronically with a PowerPoint.

3. Set the purpose for reading by instructing students to find information on two types of information in the text. This can be information that supports what has already been discussed or information that has not yet been discussed but is relevant.
4. Give students the reading selection, and ask them to predict the contents based upon the title.
5. Tell students to read the text and be prepared to discuss new information, as well as any other material from the text that is relevant to the topic.

Benefits

• Provides structure for students when reading difficult and challenging material
• Provides teacher the opportunity to pre-teach key vocabulary
• Facilitates a deeper understanding of the text
• Actively engages readers in the reading process

Considerations

• None noted.

Technology Adaptation

• Display the graphic organizer electronically.
• Ask students to email comments related to text content to teacher and classmates.

Teacher Notes

_____

_____

_____

_____

STRATEGY: QUESTIONING THE AUTHOR (QTA)

Why Use the Questioning the Author Strategy?

The purpose of the Questioning the Author strategy (Beck, McKeown, Hamilton, & Kucan, 1997) is to keep readers engaged and thinking about the information while reading a text. The questions facilitate classroom discussion for teacher and students and encourage an exchange of ideas between reader and author. This strategy is particularly beneficial to students when the reading is difficult and complex.

Types of Texts: Fiction, Nonfiction, Expository Text
This strategy can be easily modified for a variety of content areas.
Grade Level Adaptability: 5–12
Levels of Bloom's Taxonomy: Remember, Understand, Apply, Analyze, Evaluate

Steps in the Process

1. Tell students that they will be reading challenging and interesting information.
2. Display the sample questions, and model how to answer the questions while reading the material. It is helpful to have students write and respond orally with answers.
3. After students understand how to use the questions and are comfortable with the process, use the questions for discussion purposes only, as opposed to requiring an answer in writing.
4. Display questions on a PowerPoint, written on a markerboard, or provided as individual instructional guides. Questions should remain displayed for student reference throughout the time designated for reading.
5. Use professional judgment when deciding which questions to use with students. Some questions may need revising or eliminating, or additional questions may be added. The content of the questions will, to a large degree, be dependent upon the content and purpose for reading the passage in the text.

   The following are sample questions.
   - What is the main idea of the passage?
   - What are the authors trying to help you understand?
   - Why is this information important to know?
   - Did the authors explain the information clearly and succinctly?
   - What examples did the authors use to justify a specific point of view?
   - Does the author make any contradictions based on your previous knowledge of this subject?
   - How does the information in the reading "connect" with other information you already know?
   - What new information did you learn from the reading? Why is this important to understand and remember?
   - If you could ask the authors three questions, what might these be?
   - Did the author explain why it is important to understand the topic discussed in the passage? If so, please explain. If not, why do you think it is important?

6. Did the author use the structure of the text to facilitate your understanding of the content? If so, what was used? If not, what suggestions might you have for a graphic organizer or other visual aid?

Benefits

- Provides structure for students when reading difficult and challenging material
- Provides teacher flexibility with content of the questions
- Provides for differentiation among students
- Facilitates a deeper understanding of the text
- Actively engages readers in the reading process
- Helps students understand the significance of text structure
- Facilitates better preparation for reading expository material as an independent reader
- Encourages critical thinking

Considerations

- Some students may resist when required to "think" rather than merely write a response.

Technology Adaptation

- Ask students to research the author electronically related to how he lived and other things that might be pertinent to the discussion of the book.

Teacher Notes

_____

_____

_____

_____

STRATEGY: QUESTIONING CUE CARD

Why Use the Questioning Cue Card Strategy?

The purpose of the Questioning Cue Card strategy (Lenski, Wham, Johns, and Caskey, 2007) is to help students identify the main idea of a passage of text. This activity facilitates comprehension by encouraging students to be actively involved in the reading process, while identifying and rephrasing main idea statements.

Types of Texts: Fiction, Nonfiction, Expository Text
This strategy can be easily modified for a variety of content areas.
Grade Level Adaptability: 4–12
Levels of Bloom's Taxonomy: Remember, Understand

Steps in the Process

1. Tell students they will be reading informational text and ask them to brainstorm what they already know about the subject.
2. Divide students into groups of two to four.
3. Distribute index cards to each student and have them write the following:
   - *Think:* Think about the meaning of each sentence as you read it.
   - *Build:* Put your ideas about the sentences together to build meaning.
   - *Summarize:* Think of a main idea sentence about the paragraph.
   - *Question:* Change the main idea sentence into a question.
   - *Ask:* Consider possible answers to the newly written main idea question.
4. Using the aforementioned statements as the purpose for reading, give students the reading material or read each paragraph aloud.
5. After completion of the reading, ask students to think of a main idea and put the thought into sentence format.
6. After statements have been generated, ask students to change the main idea statement into a question and consider possible answers.
7. These steps continue throughout the reading of the material.

Benefits

- Provides understanding of the author's thoughts
- Facilitates careful reading and listening
- Helps students understand the importance of a main idea, as well as how to recognize it
- Facilitates understanding of difficult and challenging text
- Breaks the reading selection into manageable parts

Considerations

- This activity may be laborious and time-consuming for some students.

Technology Adaptation

- Have students answer and display the questions electronically rather than through the use of index cards.

Teacher Notes

_____

_____

_____

_____

_____

_____

STRATEGY: RECIPROCAL TEACHING

Why Use the Reciprocal Teaching Strategy?

The primary purpose of the Reciprocal Teaching strategy (Palinscar & Brown, 1996) is to help students focus and monitor their own reading in support of understanding and remembering the text.

Types of Texts: Fiction, Nonfiction, Expository Text

This strategy can be easily modified for a variety of content areas.

Grade Level Adaptability: 5–12

Levels of Bloom's Taxonomy: Remember, Understand, Apply, Analyze, Evaluate

Steps in the Process

1. Select the reading content.
2. Activate students' background knowledge by asking questions and making them predict what will be in the text.
3. Divide students into groups of three to six.
4. Direct them to read the text for the purpose of teaching the information to classmates. Explain they will take turns acting as the teacher and leading the discussion of a designated section of material.
5. Tell students that roles will then be reversed, and that they will act as the instructor by asking questions related to the reading content.
6. Tell students that each "lesson" should include predicting, clarifying, applying, analyzing, and evaluating important information from the text.

Benefits

- Provides a framework for students when reading difficult and challenging material.

- Supports careful reading of the text.
- Encourages anticipation of teacher questions about the reading content.
- Facilitates a deeper understanding of the text.
- Discourages passive participation.
- Utilizes attractive novelty through students' serving in the role of teacher.

Considerations

- Students may have difficulty formulating questions.
- The teacher will need to monitor each group closely to ensure appropriate participation.
- If few students within the group understand the text, the activity will not be productive.

Technology Adaptation

- Have students prepare and present the lesson electronically using Power-Points, e-mail, or other forms of electronic media.

Teacher Notes

_____

_____

_____

_____

_____

STRATEGY: REQUEST PROCEDURE

Why Use the ReQuest Procedure?

The ReQuest Procedure (Manzo, 1969) was designed for the purpose of encouraging students to read and reflect upon a passage by formulating questions to ask of the teacher. This technique requires students to be actively involved in the reading process. It is engaging and interesting to students because it requires them to assume the role of "teacher" while the instructor assumes the role of "student."

Types of Texts: Fiction, Nonfiction, Expository Text
This strategy can be easily modified for a variety of content areas.
Grade Level Adaptability: 4–12
Levels of Bloom's Taxonomy: Remember, Understand, Apply, Analyze, Evaluate

Steps in the Process

1. Select a reading passage and predetermine the stopping points for discussion. The stopping points should be determined by the difficulty of the material, as well as the reading abilities of the group of students. If reading comprehension is difficult for many students within the class, or if the reading content is particularly challenging, the teacher should select shorter passages. If the passage is relatively simple, longer sections can be selected. It is helpful if the stopping points are where readers can make predictions related to the upcoming passage.
2. Create a list of questions for each reading selection, ensuring that students are required to remember, understand, apply, predict, and analyze information.
3. Tell students that they will need a cover sheet to use during the lesson, and have them cover all but the title of the selection.
4. Prior to reading the assignment, ask for a volunteer to read the title aloud.
5. Based on the title of the selection, ask students to predict what will be in the passage.
6. Advise students to be ready for "role reversal," as they will assume the role of teacher; the teacher will then assume the role of student. Explain that the purpose for reading the selection is to formulate and answer questions.
7. After students have read the passage silently, allow them to pose questions.
8. After a number of students have had the opportunity to quiz the teacher, the roles reverse and the teacher asks questions of the students. When it is time to move to the next reading passage, pose the question: "What do you think will be in the next section we read?"
9. Students and teachers repeat this process until such time as the teacher believes the students can successfully read independently.

   Note: It is recommended that the teacher not always respond perfectly when students generate questions. Sometimes it is helpful to say, "You know, that is a good question, but I'm not completely sure of the answer. Does anyone else think he or she can answer the question correctly?" Or the teacher might say, "That is an excellent question. Is there anyone that can find the answer and volunteer to read it from the text to the rest of the class?"

10. While students should be asked to close their texts during the question/answer period, they should be allowed to skim for answers, if necessary.

Benefits

- Requires active participation from the reader
- Encourages reader to consider answers to the questions posed
- Requires only moderate advance preparation from the teacher
- Good activity for substitute teachers
- Encourages a positive student attitude toward strategy
- Teacher modeling of higher-level questioning and responses
- Encourages silent reading
- Helpful in classroom with students having a wide range of academic ability
- Teachers "think aloud" with students about how answers were formulated
- Works one on one, with small groups, and with the whole class
- Breaks the passage into manageable parts for students and teacher

Considerations

- The strategy may slow the reading rate of the advanced readers.
- Students may need support to ask complex and higher-order questions.

Technology Adaptation

None noted.

Teacher Notes

_____

_____

_____

_____

_____

STRATEGY: SAVE THE LAST WORD FOR ME

Why Use the Save the Last Word for Me Strategy?

The Save the Last Word for Me strategy (Rasinski & Padak, 2000) is designed to enhance student understanding of text material, as well as to foster group interaction and problem solving. Additionally, this strategy can provide a scaffold for challenging material, as well as encouraging purposeful note-taking.

Types of Texts: Fiction, Nonfiction, Expository Text

This strategy can be easily modified for a variety of content areas.

Grade Level Adaptability: 4–12

Level of Bloom's Taxonomy: Remember, Understand, Apply, Analyze, Evaluate

Steps in the Process

1. Assign students to groups of three.
2. Ask students to read all or part of the text silently.
3. Using a piece of paper, instruct them to note areas of agreement/disagreement with the author and questions that occur to them while reading.
4. Have students discuss the text with the group. Each member of the group should select a comment or question from the notecards for the purpose of discussion.
5. Ask other members of the group to react to the comment or question by sharing opinions or areas of agreement or disagreement.
6. Ask the student who initially shared the question or comment to have the "last word" by summarizing the discussion or by offering his or her own opinion.

Benefits

- Easily implemented
- Requires only moderate advance preparation from the teacher
- A good activity for a classroom with a wide range of ability
- Provides a framework for discussion of text
- Can easily be implemented with nonfiction text
- Facilitates the recognition of the main idea

Considerations

- Students need to have sufficient background information on the topic or it will be difficult for them to mentally engage with the idea of agreeing or disagreeing with the author.

- Some students may need direct instruction in appropriate ways to agree or disagree with a classmate or with ideas generated from the reading.

Technology Adaptation

- Have students use a classroom blog to post ideas related to the reading.

Teacher Notes

_____

_____

_____

_____

_____

STRATEGY: SKETCH TO STRETCH

Why Use the Sketch to Stretch Strategy?

The Sketch to Stretch strategy (Rasinski & Padak, 2004) is a nonverbal response strategy that supports visual imaging of text. This activity encourages creativity and interpretation of the reading.

Types of Texts: Fiction, Nonfiction, Expository Text

This strategy can be easily modified for a variety of content areas.

Grade Level Adaptability: 3–12

Levels of Bloom's Taxonomy: Remember, Understand, Apply, Analyze, Evaluate

Steps in the Process

1. Activate background knowledge of the students.
2. Tell students that the purpose for reading the material will be to understand and visualize the text related to important information, events, or scenes from the reading.
3. Ask students to read the text.
4. After students finish reading the text, instruct them to draw or make a quick sketch of the information. Drawings can include a scene, the main idea, or other pertinent information.

5. When students have completed their sketches, give them the opportunity to interpret each drawing. This can be done in writing, using sticky notes, or verbally, during whole-class or small-group discussion.

6. After students have provided interpretations, ask the illustrator to explain the drawing to the whole class.

Benefits

- Easily implemented
- Requires only moderate advance preparation from the teacher
- Good activity for substitute teachers
- Supports mental imaging of content
- Provides a framework for discussion of text
- Can easily be implemented with nonfiction text
- Works with individual or with small groups of students

Considerations

- Elementary students are sometimes less inhibited than secondary students related to drawing or sketching ideas. Secondary students can be encouraged by teacher emphasis on content of the drawing, rather than the artistic ability of the illustrator.

Technology Adaptation

- Have students scan sketches or drawings into a computer and display them visually for whole-class comments.
- Have students post scanned documents on a classroom website or blog for students to add comments or observations.
- Have students get visual images from an electronic source and create a multimedia collage of the information.

Teacher Notes

_____

_____

_____

_____

_____

STRATEGY: STORY IMPRESSIONS

Why Use the Story Impressions Strategy?

The purpose of the Story Impressions strategy (McGinley & Denner, 1985) is to provide a pre-writing activity that supports reading comprehension and vocabulary development. This strategy will support readers by actively engaging them while thinking about ideas as part of an anticipatory set.

Types of Texts: Fiction

Grade Level Adaptability: Grades 2–12

Levels of Bloom's Taxonomy: Remember, Understand, Apply, Analyze

Steps in the Process

1. Activate background knowledge by introducing the story.
2. Provide a listing of words, phrases, or clues that are key to the understanding of the text. The order of the word listing should correspond with the storyline.
3. After students have read the words, ask them to brainstorm how the words may be connected in the story. Students can work individually, in small groups, or as a whole class.
4. Explain to students the purpose for reading is to determine how closely their predictions were to the content of the text.
5. Students or teachers should record impressions of students on paper.

Benefits

- Encourages student engagement
- Novel anticipatory set for lesson
- Good activity for a class having a wide range of reading ability
- Encourages interdependence within the classroom
- Supports retention of material
- Facilitates prediction related to the reading selection
- Encourages critical thinking
- Establishes a purpose for reading

Considerations

- Teacher preparation time is needed to formulate important words and/or phrases.

Technology Adaptation

- Display predictions and impressions electronically to the whole class.

Teacher Notes

_____

_____

_____

_____

_____

STRATEGY: TEXT STRUCTURE

Why Use Text Structure Strategy?

Using Text Structure strategy (Tierney and Readance, 2000) helps students understand how to use features within a text to facilitate understanding and recall of information. While narrative texts usually have a consistent structure, a nonfiction text may have more variety in terms of format.

Types of Texts: Nonfiction, Expository Text

This strategy can be easily modified for a variety of content areas.

Grade Level Adaptability: 4–12

Levels of Bloom's Taxonomy: Remember, Understand, Apply

Steps in the Process

1. At the beginning of the lesson, tell students that authors use the structure of a text to facilitate understanding. Explain that if they don't understand the significance of these features or how to use them advantageously, they may have difficulty focusing, monitoring, and understanding written material.
2. Ask students to divide notebook paper into three equal vertical columns. Tell them to write "Text Structure" at the top of the column on the left, and "Example" at the top of the middle column. Tell them to write "How This Helps" at the top of the column on the right side of the paper.
3. Ask students to complete the organizer by locating the specific support, giving an example of the support, and explaining how the support helps with comprehension. Sample supports include, but are not limited to, the following:
   • Chapter title
   • Headings
   • Subheadings

- Photos
- Bold print
- Italics
- Diagrams
- Graphic organizers
- Author questions
- Key vocabulary

4. After students have had experience with the graphic organizer for text structures, it may only be necessary to have them discuss the features of an upcoming chapter as a whole-class experience.

   Note: It is recommended that students receive instruction in how to use the text structure throughout the school year, using each assigned textbook. This instruction can also be modified for reading material presented online.

Benefits

- Helps students understand the significance of a variety of features on a printed page
- Helps ensure that all students have the same level of advantage when reading difficult text
- Facilitates better preparation for reading expository material as an independent reader
- Can be done individually, with small groups, or with the whole class

Considerations

- Without the appropriate teacher emphasis, some students will underestimate the importance of text structure related to reading comprehension.

Technology Adaptation

- Have students find an article on the Internet and evaluate the structures provided. Explain that many of the same features are used with Internet articles—that is, color, font size, bold print, graphics, and so forth.

Teacher Notes

_____

_____

_____

_____

STRATEGY: THAT WAS THEN . . . THIS IS NOW

Why Use the That Was Then . . . This Is Now Strategy?

The That Was Then . . . This Is Now strategy (McLaughlin & Allen, 2002) was designed to encourage students to think about what they already know, relate the information to what they read from a text, and to visualize the text content.

Types of Texts: Fiction, Nonfiction, Expository Text

This strategy can be easily modified for a variety of content areas.

Grade Level Adaptability: 3–12

Levels of Bloom's Taxonomy: Remember, Understand, Apply

Steps in the Process

1. Identify a topic and introduce it to the students.
2. Divide students into groups of three to four.
3. Ask students to draw a vertical line in the center of a sheet of paper.
4. At the top of the column on the left, ask students to write the words "That was then . . ."
5. At the top of the column on the right, ask students to write the words ". . . this is now."
6. In the column on the left, ask students to draw some of the things they already know about the topic.
7. At the bottom of the left side of the paper tell students to write a summary statement. This statement can be tied to the drawing, or it can provide supplemental information.
8. Ask students to read the text.
9. After completing the reading assignment, instruct students to draw a representation of what they learned from the reading in the column on the right.
10. Tell them to write a summary statement under the column on the right.
11. Ask students to compare and contrast the before and after sketches with a partner, with other groups, or with the whole class.

Benefits

- Can be done individually or with a small group
- Encourages creativity
- Requires only moderate advance preparation from the teacher
- Novel method of activating background knowledge
- Facilitates mental imaging
- Helpful in classroom with students having a wide range of academic ability
- Requires students to compare and contrast information

Considerations

- Some students may resist due to a perceived lack of skill related to drawing and sketching.
- Students will need some background knowledge of the topic prior to beginning the assignment.

Technology Adaptation

- Have students use electronic images to design the visual product.

Teacher Notes

_____

_____

_____

_____

STRATEGY: THINK, PREDICT, READ, AND CONNECT

Why Use the Think, Predict, Read, and Connect Strategy?

The purpose of the Think, Predict, Read, and Connect strategy (Ruddell, 2005) is to help students develop general knowledge before, during, and after reading.

Types of Texts: Fiction, Nonfiction, Expository Text

This strategy can be easily modified for a variety of content areas.

Grade Level Adaptability: 4–12

Levels of Bloom's Taxonomy: Remember, Understand, Apply, Analyze, Evaluate

Steps in the Process

1. Explain to students the topic for the lesson while activating their background knowledge.
2. Divide the students into groups of three to four.
3. Using notebook or larger sheets of paper, ask students to write the topic at the top. Using vertical lines, tell students to divide the paper into three equal sections.
4. At the top of the left column, ask students to write the word "Think." At the top of the middle column, ask them to write the word "Predict." At the top of the right column, have them write the word "Connect."

5. Ask students to think about what they already know about the topic. This information should be recorded in the "Think" column.
6. After explaining to students that they will be reading information on this topic, ask them to review what was written in the "Think" column and place a checkmark in the "Predict" column beside the information they believe will be included in the text.
7. Ask students to read the selection and mark with a sticky note or highlight the text, if it includes information they predicted would be included.
8. Have students make connections between the information in the text and what they already know about the topic as they read. Have them record these thoughts in the "Connect" column.

Benefits

- Provides structure for reading
- Activates background knowledge
- Provides critical information for the teacher about students' preconceived knowledge
- Straightforward, easy to explain and understand
- Helpful tool for students to use when reading independently
- Can be done individually or with small groups

Considerations

- It is a difficult activity to facilitate if students have little prior knowledge of topic.
- It may be difficult for students to "Connect" if they lack background knowledge.
- Teacher modeling of possible answers may be necessary.

Technology Adaptation

- Ask students to create an electronic graphic organizer and fill in each column. Students should be prepared to show the whole class the organizer while facilitating a discussion of the contents.

Teacher Notes

_____

_____

_____

_____

STRATEGY: TOSS UP

Why Use the Toss Up Strategy?

The Toss Up strategy was designed to encourage students to think about what they learned from the text and to summarize ideas and content.

Types of Texts: Fiction, Nonfiction, Expository Text

This strategy can be easily modified for a variety of content areas.

Grade Level Adaptability: 4–12

Levels of Bloom's Taxonomy: Remember, Understand, Apply, Analyze, Evaluate

Steps in the Process

1. Develop questions from the reading passage that reflect all levels of Bloom's Taxonomy.
2. After students have finished reading a selected passage, ask them to stand in a circle.
3. Tell students they will be tossing a ball to each other. Each student will get 1 point for catching the ball and 2 points for supplying the correct answer to a question.
4. Using some type of soft ball, gently toss the ball to a student and ask a question from the reading.
5. The game continues until all students have had the opportunity to participate by tossing the ball and answering questions.

Benefits

- Novel activity
- Provides students the opportunity for physical movement
- Competition encouraged
- Requires moderate advance preparation from the teacher
- Good activity as closure or review for a more formal assessment
- Activity can be done outdoors

Considerations

- Classroom management skills need to be evident.
- Some students will need to be taught how to politely participate in the activity.

Technology Adaptation

None noted.

Teacher Notes

_____

_____

_____

_____

STRATEGY: UNSENT LETTERS

Why Use the Unsent Letters Strategy?

The purpose of the Unsent Letters strategy (Vacca & Vaca, 2008) is to reflect upon and personally connect and understand a reading selection.

Types of Texts: Fiction, Nonfiction, Expository Text

This strategy can be easily modified for a variety of content areas.

Grade Level Adaptability: 4–12

Levels of Bloom's Taxonomy: Remember, Understand, Apply, Analyze

Steps in the Process

1. Tell students that they will write a letter to someone about an issue or situation they have recently studied. If necessary, offer options or choices for students.
2. Ask students to review the information from the textbook, as well as notes from class discussions.
3. Instruct students to chose an individual and write a letter to that person that reflects an understanding of the topic, issue, or events. Explain the writing should reflect interpretation, analysis, or evaluation of the topic. Encourage creativity.

Benefits

- Straightforward, easy to explain and understand
- Encourages creativity
- Provides for differentiation depending upon choice of letter recipient or other factors related to the reading selection

Considerations

- Teacher modeling of a letter may help some students begin the assignment.

Technology Adaptation

• Ask students to e-mail classmates and the teacher the "Unsent Letter."

Teacher Notes

_____

_____

_____

_____

_____

Chapter 3

Helping Students Help Themselves

It is not uncommon to hear educators and those in the business community discuss the types of skills young people need to have when entering the workforce. While many of these conversations cite the need for basic skills, some also include references to lifelong learning, the ability to solve difficult and complex problems, and critical thinking.

A common recommendation from educators to students and parents is that individuals need to study harder. For many students, this is an oversimplification. It is usually not a matter of studying "harder" but rather the recognition of the need to change the type of study method.

The strategies and information presented in this section are intended to help students help themselves when a teacher or mentor is not present to guide and assist. Most suggestions can be implemented easily and with little effort, but some will require students to rethink their habits related to studying and learning new information.

The following pages will include suggestions for students related to studying smarter. The reader will notice that the content is written directly to students, and in a conversational tone. This is done purposely, for good reason.

The information can be taught directly, as part of a lesson, or discussed and reinforced as part of the daily dialogue between teacher and students. Either way, it is critically important that students understand and internalize the information, as well as use the suggestions in their own best interest.

STUDYING SMART

A number of strategies and techniques can help students efficiently and correctly complete assignments. The following Instant Study Skills (Wark, 2007) provide effective suggestions in terms of time and effort.

- Sit in the front of the classroom. When seated in the front of the classroom, there are fewer distractions and temptations in terms of off-task behavior. Though many teachers use seating charts and assign seating based upon a variety of factors, most will accommodate a request to sit in the front so long as they believe it is made for legitimate reasons.
- Routinely review previous class notes. This can be done before or after class, or even during class when the student believes it is beneficial to do so. Repetition supports learning. Periodically reviewing notes throughout the instructional unit will facilitate retention of content.
- Copy important points from the whiteboard or PowerPoint. If the instructor believes the information is important enough to display to the class, assume that the information might appear again in the form of an assessment instrument.
- Find a place that is conducive to studying, and consistently use it to do so. Individuals are creatures of habit. Good habits related to studying routines and rituals are important. Finding a location used primarily for the purpose of completing homework is a good first step in terms of task accomplishment.
- Set goals and determine a time for assignment completion. Giving thought to how much time a task will take helps with time management. By virtue of their complexity, some projects take longer to complete than others. Break assignments into manageable times, and maintain the self-discipline needed to start and finish in a timely manner.
- When bored or distracted during study time, briefly set aside the assignment. Stand, walk around the room, or eat something sweet—just remember to not overuse this strategy by applying it at every initial sign of fatigue.
- Self-quiz when reading difficult and complex texts. Stop at the bottom of a page and ask what has been learned. Summarize the important points. Take notes or underline.
- Don't try to read too quickly. It is easy to be discouraged and think that an assignment will never be finished. Depending upon the purpose, good readers know that their rate of reading may need adjustment. If you will be held accountable for the information, read slowly and concentrate carefully on content. Reading in short spurts can help combat fatigue and concentration.
- Do a first review at the end of the reading session. Before putting the text away at the end of a study period, take time to quickly flip through the pages while looking at highlighted material, bold or italicized print, graphics, and captions. This is a good way to provide closure to the activity and support retention.

- When an assignment is finished ahead of schedule, personal rewards help facilitate a positive attitude. The mental outlook brought to a study session is important to success, so think positively. Few individuals enjoy expending long hours of concentration and effort on academic tasks, but most appreciate the feelings that come from accomplishing the assignment in a reasonable amount of time.
- Avoid underlining or highlighting an entire sentence or paragraph within a text. While underlining and highlighting can be helpful to retention, use these techniques sparingly, and after finishing the first reading of the material. This will serve as the first review of the content.
- When taking a test, complete the easy questions first. This helps build confidence and can even provide hints to possible answers for more difficult testing items.
- On an essay exam, do not leave any question unanswered. When an item is left totally blank, a teacher has no choice but to assign a zero. Write *something*.
- When taking a test, be careful to use good handwriting. Nothing is more frustrating for a teacher than struggling to read a student's handwriting. Grading papers and tests is time-consuming enough without the added stress of trying to decipher poor penmanship. Do not have an answer marked as wrong because the teacher could not read what was written.
- On objective tests, do not hesitate to change an answer if warranted. The idea that the first choice that occurs to you is usually the correct one may not always be true. There are a number of reasons why you might need to modify an answer: Perhaps something is triggered in your subconscious mind. Maybe another question gives a hint about the actual correct answer. Changing a previously recorded answer may be a good move if the situation warrants it.

CONCENTRATION IS CRITICAL

Few would argue that studying effectively requires effort and concentration. Consequently, recognize when attention is starting to weaken, and work to regain your focus.

A number of factors can interfere with the ability to concentrate, including fatigue, stress, irritation, lack of organizational skills, and poor study habits.

Possible Solutions

- Trying to study late into the evening seldom gives much of a return in terms of retention. The best time to study is immediately after school. At that time of day, it is easier to be in a school mindset, and easier also to remember directions and lesson content. If other commitments keep you from studying in the afternoon, study as soon as possible after the conclusion of the school day.

- Preview the structure of the text prior to beginning any reading assignment. It only takes a few minutes to survey a chapter and note its headings, subheadings, titles, graphics, and bold or italicized print. Remember that the author uses text structure to communicate what is important as well as to activate background knowledge on a topic.

- Immediately rereading a text may not yield maximal learning. In terms of time spent, taking notes is more supportive of the overall understanding of material. If rereading is necessary, approach the material differently by turning headings into questions or by first reading the conclusions.

- Wait to take notes over a text until the end of a section. Stopping and starting reading in an attempt to take notes can interfere with your ability to stay focused. Read to the end of the section, then make notes or highlight the text.

- Remember that underlining and highlighting do not support retention as well as writing down notes. Summarizing an author's thoughts or ideas requires a more active mind.

- Do not wait to be in the mood for studying. Only rarely will people feel like doing homework. If you are waiting on inspiration or the proper mood, the task may never be completed.

- Be in the habit of studying at a set time and location. The activities most conducive to learning work best when accompanied by the appropriate habit.

- If the content of the text is challenging, find something easier to read on the same subject. Read the easier material first—taking time to read a related text may help build confidence and activate background knowledge. With the use of the Internet, this is no longer a difficult or time-consuming task.

- Be aware of noise and the surrounding environment. It is not possible to focus on more than one thing at a time. If a television or loud music is in the background, it will interfere with concentration. As a result, a relatively short homework assignment may become a lengthy and painful experience when there is an abundance of unnecessary visual or auditory stimulation.

- Do not study in bed. If the assignment is less than novel or interesting, it will be difficult to remain awake. Sitting at a table with a chair that resembles a student desk will keep the mindset of academics in place.

- When it is necessary to study for an exam and time is in short supply, learn the associated vocabulary words. Though knowing vocabulary alone does not guarantee the best possible grade, it may result in a passing rather failing grade.

- Read test directions carefully. No one wants to miss an item on a test due to carelessness.
- Understand why the information is valuable. If this seems impossible to do, ask the teacher for assistance. Content specialists should be able to provide both short- and long-term benefits of learning an instructional objective.
- Recognize that reading rate varies, and that the variation is not necessarily a bad thing. Complex vocabulary and other factors require that some subjects be read more slowly. Nonfiction texts, in particular, can be difficult for many readers. World geography, science, and foreign languages are examples of content areas that require most readers to read, pause, and reflect.
- Use flash cards, vocabulary cards, and term cards. When asked to remember new terminology, use repetition. Whether through the use of a self-quiz or using the cards with a study 'buddy,' flash cards can be beneficial. When self-quizzing, say answers aloud. This strategy will help learners who have a strong auditory memory.
- When studying for a test, try to anticipate possible questions. Write answers, and work with a friend to review and quiz. Ask the teacher how he or she would recommend studying for the exam. Seek clarification about the number of true/false, multiple-choice, essay, and short answer questions that will be included.
- When reviewing for an exam, divide a piece of paper vertically. In the left column write possible questions. In the right column, record possible answers. When it is time to study the notes, fold the paper from right to left, covering the answers. Self quiz. If the answer does not come to mind, unfold the paper the paper and read the answer out loud.
- When taking notes on a book or in a class, skip lines between ideas and/or topics. This makes the print more pleasing to the eye and allows room for modifications and additions.
- Resist doodling on notes. Drawing unrelated pictures can be distracting and will make it difficult to actively listen during a lecture. If the mind starts to wander, look back through previous notes. At the very least, this keeps the topic in mind.
- Read the author's questions prior to beginning to read a text. The questions may be at the beginning or the end of the chapter, or even be in the margins. Regardless, questions help develop a purpose for reading the material.
- Avoid procrastination. Everyone does it occasionally—some routinely. Regardless, procrastination is a habit that should be broken, entirely avoided.
- Keep a personal calendar. Tracking assignments, due dates, and personal schedules can be advantageous to time management.

- Begin studying for the exam from the first day of class by frequently reviewing material. This will help place the information into long-term memory as well as minimizing test anxiety.
- When reading, monitor comprehension. At any time the reading becomes a passive activity, regroup and refocus.
- Get plenty of rest and proper nutrition. Easier said than done, to be sure, but both are invaluable when it comes to learning.
- Be familiar with how to effectively use "fix-up strategies." Fix-up strategies are techniques used by good readers when encountering an unfamiliar term or phrase. Common fix-up strategies include phonetic analysis, contextual analysis, structural analysis, glossaries, dictionaries, or skipping the word or phrase entirely.
- If the teacher does not provide a specific purpose for reading, set your own purpose. Suggested purposes might include the following:
  - Pretend you are the teacher and write 5–10 possible test questions (with answers) from the text.
  - Remember five to seven things you learned that you did not know prior to the reading. Make a listing, and rank them according to importance.
  - Make five to seven personal connections to the reading content. Imagine how you might explain these connections to a friend.
  - Imagine that you are going to have to teach the most important points from the reading to a classmate. What information would you want to include in the lesson?
  - Survey the content, and make note of the author's use of text structure. Which words are italicized, in bold font, or included in headings? Why are these words given a special notation? How does the meaning of those words affect the content of the reading selection?
  - Locate important vocabulary words, and make a listing of the words, including a definition.
- Become familiar with the school and public library. While the Internet has brought many resources into the home, do not underestimate the expertise of the library media specialist. These individuals can help streamline research and provide a variety of educational resources that might otherwise be unknown to many students.
- Monitor listening skills, and refocus when necessary. Prepare for listening by having a personal "pep talk." Question what a speaker may say. Challenge ideas, analyze, and make personal connections.
- Use both graphics and words when taking notes during a lecture or from a text. A visual representation of a concept can help learners simplify and visualize complex information.

References

Allen, J. (1999). *Words, words, words: Teaching vocabulary in grades 4–12.* York, ME: Stenhouse.

Allen, J. (2007). *Inside words: Tools for teaching academic vocabulary grades 4–12.* Portland, ME: Stenhouse.

Anderson, L. W. & Krathwohl, D. R. (eds.). (2001). *A taxonomy for learning, teaching and assessing: A revision of Bloom's taxonomy of educational objectives.* (complete ed.). New York: Longman.

Beck, I. L., McKeown, M. G., Hamilton, R. L., & Kucan, L. (1997). *Questioning the author: An approach for enhancing student engagement with text.* Newark, DE: International Reading Association.

Blachowicz, C. L. Z. (1986). Making connections: Alternatives to the vocabulary notebook. *Journal of Reading, 29,* 539–543.

Buehl, D. R. (2001). *Classroom strategies for interactive learning.* (2nd ed.). Newark, DE: International Reading Association.

Brunner, Judy. (2009). These Kids Can't Read. *Principal Leadership, 9,* 19–22.

Dana, C. & Rodriguez, M. (1992). TOAST: A system to study vocabulary. *Reading Research and Instruction, 31,* 78–84.

Davidson, J. (1982). The group mapping activity for instruction in reading and thinking. *Journal of Reading, 26,* 52–56.

De Bono, E. (1994). *De Bono's Thinking Course.* (rev. ed.). New York: Barnes & Noble Books.

Denner, P. R. & McGinley, W. J. (1986). The effects of story-impressions as a pre-reading/writing activity on story comprehension. *Journal of Educational Research, 82,* 320–326.

Gillet, J. & Kita, M. J. (1979). Words, kids, and categories. *The Reading Teacher, 32,* 538–546.

Graves, D. & Hansen, J. (1993). The author's chair. *Language Arts, 60,* 176–183.

Haggard, M. (1986). The vocabulary self-collection strategy: Using student interest and world knowledge to enhance vocabulary growth. *Journal of Reading, 29,* 634–642.

Klemp, R. (1994). Word storm: Connecting vocabulary to the students' database. *The Reading Teacher, 48,* 282.

Langer, J. A. (1981). From theory to practice: A prereading plan. *Journal of Reading, 25,* 152–156.

Lenski, S., Wham, M. A., Johns, J. L., & Caskey, M. M. (2007). *Reading and learning strategies: Middle grades through high school.* (3rd ed.). Dubuque, IA: Kendall/Hunt.

Longman Dictionary of American English (3rd ed.). 2004. Harlow, Essex, England: Pearson Education Ltd.

Lubliner, S. (2004). Help for struggling upper-grade elementary readers. *The Reading Teacher, 57,* 430–438.

Manzo, A. (1969). The request procedure. *Journal of Reading, 13,* 23–26.

Marzano, R. (2004). *Building background knowledge for academic achievement: Research on what works in schools.* Alexandria, VA: Association for Supervision and Curriculum Development.

McLaughlin, M. & Allen, M. B. (2002). *Guided comprehension: A teaching model for grades 3–8.* Newark, DE: International Reading Association.

Moore, D. W. & Moore, S. A. (1992). Possible sentences: An update. In E. K. Dishner, T. W. Bean, J. E. Readence, & D. W. Moore (eds.), *Reading in the content areas: Improving classroom instruction* (3rd ed.) (196–202). Dubuque, IA: Kendall/Hunt.

Palinscar, A. M. & Brown, A. (1986). Interactive teaching to promote independent learning from text. *The Reading Teacher, 39*(8), 771–777.

Pauk, W. (1974). *How to study in college.* Boston: Houghton Mifflin.

Oczkus, L. (2004). *Super six comprehension strategies: 35 lessons and more for reading success.* Norwood, MA: Christopher-Gordon.

Ogle, D. (1986). K-W-L: A teaching model that develops active reading of expository text. *The Reading Teacher, 39,* 564–570.

Rasinski, T. & Padak, N. (1996). *Holistic reading strategies: Teaching children who find reading difficult.* Englewood Cliffs, NJ: Merrill/Prentice Hall.

Readance, J., Bean, T., & Baldwin, R. (1998). *Content area literacy: An integrated approach.* (6th ed.). Dubuque, IA: Kendall/Hunt.

Rogers, T. (1991). Students as literary critics: The interpretative experiences, beliefs, and processes of ninth grade students. *Journal of Reading Behavior, 23*(4), 391–423.

Rosenbaum, C. (2001). A word map for middle schools: A tool for effective vocabulary instruction. *Journal of Adolescent & Adult Literacy, 45,* 44–49.

Ruddell, M. (2005). *Teaching content area reading and writing.* (4th ed.). Hoboken, NJ: John Wiley & Sons.

Schwartz, R., and Raphael, T. (1985). Concept of definition: A key to improving students' vocabulary. *The Reading Teacher, 39,* 198–205.

Slavir, R. (1994). *Educational psychology: Theory and practice.* Boston: Allyn and Bacon.

Steele, J., Meredith, K., & Temple, C. (1998). *Further strategies for promoting critical thinking: Guidebook IV.* Prepared for the Reading & Writing for Critical Thinking Project, a joint collaboration with University of Northern Iowa, International Reading Association, and the Open Society Institute.

Taba, H. (1967). *Teacher's handbook for elementary social studies.* Reading, MS: Addison Wesley.

Tierney, R. & Readance, J. (2000). *Reading strategies and practices: A compendium.* (5th ed.). Boston: Allyn & Bacon.

Unrau, N. (2004). *Content area reading and writing: Fostering literacies in middle and high school cultures.* Upper Saddle River, NJ: Merrill Prentice Hall.

Vacca, R. T. & Vacca, J. L. (2008). *Content area reading: Literacy and learning across the curriculum.* (9th ed.). Boston: Allyn & Bacon.

Wark, D. M. (2007). *General Study Skills: Instant Study Skills.* University of Minnesota Counseling & Consulting Services, http://www.uccs.umn.edu/counseling/self_service/study_general.htm.

About the Author

Judy Marie Tilton Brunner is a consultant and cofounder of Edu-Safe and Instructional Solutions Group. She has worked in public and private education as a reading and special education teacher and as an elementary, middle, and high school principal. She currently serves as part of the clinical faculty at Missouri State University.

428.43 B897   INFCW

Brunner, Judy Tilton,

I don't get it! :helping students

understand what they read /
CENTRAL LIBRARY

10/12